# Copycat Recipes Vol. 2

# Making Restaurants' Most Popular Recipes at Home

## Lina Chang

## Copyrights

## Disclaimer and Terms of Use

Effort has been made to ensure that the information in this book is accurate and complete. However, the author and the publisher do not warrant the accuracy of the information, text, and graphics contained within the book due to the rapidly changing nature of science, research, known and unknown facts, and internet. The author and the publisher do not hold any responsibility for errors, omissions, or contrary interpretation of the subject matter herein. This book is presented solely for motivational and informational purposes only.

The recipes provided in this book are for informational purposes only and are not intended to provide dietary advice. A medical practitioner should be consulted before making any changes in diet. Additionally, recipe cooking times may require adjustment depending on age and quality of appliances. Readers are strongly urged to take all precautions to ensure ingredients are fully cooked in order to avoid the dangers of foodborne illnesses. The recipes and suggestions provided in this book are solely the opinion of the author. The author and publisher do not take any responsibility for any consequences that may result due to following the instructions provided in this book.

*ISBN: 978-1978431386*

*Printed in the United States*

—— THE ——
COOK🍳BOOK
PUBLISHER

# Contents

# Introduction

Everyone likes to dine out every once in a while—a date night with a significant other, a family dinner at a nice restaurant, lunch out or coffee with friends at a local café, or even a quick drive-by at a favorite fast food place. There's just something about eating out that, whether alone or with company, makes eating all the more enjoyable. Maybe you think that you'll never be able to recreate the food you order at Outback Steakhouse, Starbucks, Chipotle, or Applebee's. So, you go in there, wait in line for what seems like an eternity, and then pay for food that you know is way overpriced. But what if you didn't have to go through all that? What if you could be munching on your favorite dessert you made right in your own home? No leaving the house, no waiting in line, and no spending money on expensive food—just the amazing taste of your beloved restaurant dishes and the satisfaction that you were able to recreate them all by yourself (or with friends or family). And, with the help of this cookbook, you'll be able to do just that in no time. The main objective of this Copycat series is to bring you kitchen-tested recipes that taste just like the ones in your favorite restaurant. This cookbook is the second volume in this series. In it you will discover even more of your favorite recipes from well-known restaurants from all over America.

## The Cost of Eating Out

When you pay for a meal at a restaurant, usually you're paying three times more than the actual cost of the ingredients it took to make the food. That's around $14 in a restaurant which would have only cost $4.25 if you had made it yourself. There are four ways restaurant owners price their menu items. The first method is based on this equation: "cost of raw ingredients" divided by "desired food cost percentage (which is about 25-30%)" equals "the price." This is how the $14 restaurant meal cost was calculated earlier.

The second method is to base the price on competing restaurants. Restaurant owners will either adopt the same price of their competitors, lower the price of their meals for those trying to find a better deal, or raise their prices to appear of higher quality compared to their competition.

The third method of menu pricing is to base prices on supply and demand. For example, the food is usually priced higher at places like sports stadiums and airports simply because they know you will be hungry and/or thirsty and there aren't a lot of other options. Restaurants that have unique themes to their interior or food can also mark their prices higher since the customers aren't just paying for the food, they're also paying for the overall dining experience.

Finally, the fourth and last pricing method is by evaluating your menu items' profitability. If restaurant owners know that one particular meal is selling well, they will raise the other prices by just a small, infinitesimal amount so that it will increase profitability to balance with the best-sellers. Regardless of the pricing method, when you're eating at a restaurant, you're not just paying for the food but for the restaurants overhead as well.

This cookbook is filled with even more copycat recipes from your favorite restaurants that you can make at home, some as quick as 30 minutes. There are over 100 recipes ranging from breakfast meals and snacks to entrees, sides, and desserts to choose from. You'll start cooking like a restaurant chef in no time!

# Copycat Breakfast Recipes

## IHOP's Buttermilk Pancake

There has always been something special about IHOP pancakes. If you want a quick and scrumptious breakfast, here is a recipe that will surely satisfy your taste buds.

*Serves: 8 to 10 – Preparation Time: 5 minutes – Cooking Time: 8 minutes*
*Nutrition facts per serving: Calories 180.1, Total Fat 7.9 g, Carbs 23.2 g, Protein 4.1 g, Sodium 271.6 mg*

### Ingredients
1¼ cups all-purpose flour
1 teaspoon baking soda
1 teaspoon baking powder
1¼ cups granulated sugar
1 pinch salt
1 egg
1¼ cups buttermilk
¼ cup cooking oil

## Preparation

1. Preheat your pan by leaving it over medium heat while you are preparing the pancake batter.
2. Take all of your dry ingredients and mix them together.
3. Take all of your wet ingredients and mix them together.
4. Carefully combine the dry mixture into the wet mixture until everything is mixed together completely.
5. Melt some butter in your pan.
6. Slowly pour batter into the pan until you have a 5-inch circle.
7. Flip the pancake when its edges seem to have hardened.
8. Cook the other side of the pancake until it is golden brown.
9. Repeat steps six through eight until your batter is finished.
10. Serve with softened butter and maple syrup.

# McDonald's Breakfast Burrito

Prepare a simple McDonald's Burrito to complete your morning routine.

*Serves: 10 – Preparation Time: 10 minutes – Cooking Time: 16 minutes*
*Nutrition facts per serving: Calories 270.1, Total Fat 14.8 g, Carbs 18.2 g,*
*Protein 15.2 g, Sodium 525.3 mg*

## Ingredients
½ pound bulk sausage, cooked, crumbled
10 eggs, scrambled
1 medium tomato, diced
1 small onion, diced
3 tablespoons canned green chili, diced
Some salt and pepper
10 flour tortillas, warm
10 slices American cheese, halved
Some salsa
Some sour cream

### Preparation

1. Mix the first six ingredients together in a medium-sized bowl.
2. Butter a non-stick pan over medium heat.
3. Pour the mixture into the pan and then cook until the egg is cooked the way you like.
4. When the mixture has reached your desired consistency, take it off the heat.
5. Lay out the tortillas and start assembling your burritos by placing one-tenth of the mixture in each of the tortillas.
6. Place the cheese on top of the egg mixture, then roll up the tortilla to make the burrito.
7. Garnish the roll with salsa and sour cream and serve.

# Starbucks's Marble Pound Cake

Sometimes, sugar is essential to get that blood pumping in the morning. Make this pound cake the night before and have a slice before you go to work.

*Serves: 16 – Preparation Time: 10 minutes – Cooking Time: 1 hour 30 min.*
*Nutrition facts per serving: Calories 582.1, Total Fat 32 g, Carbs 69.6 g,*
*Protein 8.6 g, Sodium 114.8 mg*

## Ingredients
4½ cups cake flour
2 teaspoons baking powder
⅛ teaspoon salt
6 ounces semisweet chocolate, finely chopped
2 cups unsalted butter, softened
3 cups granulated sugar
1 tablespoon vanilla
1 lemon, grated for zest
10 large eggs
2 tablespoons orange liquor OR milk

## Preparation

1. Assemble your ingredients, and then:
   a) Preheat the oven to 350°F;
   b) Grease a 10×4-inch tube pan;
   c) Line the pan's bottom with greased wax paper; and
   d) Flour the entire pan.
2. Sift together the cake flour, baking powder, and salt in a medium-sized bowl—this is your dry mixture.
3. Melt the chocolate in a medium-sized bowl, then beat in the butter. When the mixture is smooth, beat in the sugar, lemon zest, and vanilla until the liquid mixture is uniform.
4. When the mixture is fully beaten, beat in the eggs, two at a time, until the mixture looks curdled.
5. Pour half of your dry mixture into your liquid mixture and mix until blended.
6. Add the orange liquor and the rest of the dry mixture. Continue beating the mixture.
7. When the mixture is blended, use a spatula to start folding it—this is your batter.
8. Set aside 4 cups of the batter. Whisk the melted chocolate into the remaining batter.
9. Now that you have a light batter and a dark batter, place the batter into the tube pan by the spoonful, alternating between the two colors.
10. When the pan is full, shake it slightly to level the batter. Run a knife through the batter to marble it.
11. Place the pan in the oven and bake for an hour and 15 minutes. To test if the cake is done, poke it with a toothpick. If there are still some moist crumbs on the toothpick when you take it out, then the cake is done.
12. Remove the cake from the pan and leave it to rest overnight.

# IHOP's Scrambled Egg

Scrambled eggs are a classic breakfast dish. This dish is a simple yet delicious upgrade to your normal breakfast eggs.

*Serves: 4 – Preparation Time: 5 minutes – Cooking Time: 5 minutes*
*Nutrition facts per serving: Calories 870, Total Fat 54 g, Carbs 9 g,*
*Protein 69 g, Sodium 34.9 mg*

## Ingredients
¼ cup pancake mix
1–2 tablespoons butter
6 large eggs
Salt and pepper, to taste

## Preparation

1. Thoroughly beat the pancake mix and the eggs together until no lumps or clumps remain.
2. Butter a pan over medium heat.
3. When the pan is hot enough, pour the egg mixture in the middle of the pan.
4. Add the salt and pepper and let the mixture sit for about a minute.
5. When the egg starts cooking, start pushing the edges of the mixture toward the middle of the pan. Continue until the entire mixture is cooked.
6. Serve and enjoy.

# McDonald's' Fruit and Yogurt Parfait

No need to go to McDonald's to get that yummy fruit and yogurt parfait. Make one at home and eat it before starting your day.

*Serves: 10 – Preparation Time: 5 minutes – Cooking Time: n/a*
*Nutrition facts per serving: Calories 328.9, Total Fat 25.4 g, Carbs 20.7 g,*
*Protein 9 g, Sodium 79.7 mg*

## Ingredients
6 ounces vanilla yogurt, divided into 3
4–6 strawberries, sliced
¼ cup blueberries, fresh or frozen; divided into 2
¼ cup pecans, chopped; divided into 2

## *Preparation*

1. Place 2 ounces of vanilla yogurt at the bottom of a cup, followed by 2–3 strawberries and ⅛ cup each of blueberries and pecans.
2. Place another layer of yogurt, strawberries, blueberries, and pecans on top of the first layer.
3. Finish off the parfait with the remaining yogurt—you can garnish it with more fruits if you like.

# Starbucks's Chocolate Cinnamon Bread

If you feel like having something sweet to start your day, then this yummy chocolate bread may be just what you've been looking for.

*Serves: 16 – Preparation Time: 15 minutes – Cooking Time: 1 hour*
*Nutrition facts per serving: Calories 370, Total Fat 14 g, Carbs 59 g,*
*Protein 7 g, Sodium 270 mg*

## *Ingredients*
Bread:
1½ cups unsalted butter
3 cups granulated sugar
5 large eggs
2 cups flour
1¼ cups processed cocoa
1 tablespoon ground cinnamon
1 teaspoon salt
½ teaspoon baking powder

½ teaspoon baking soda
¼ cup water
1 cup buttermilk
1 teaspoon vanilla extract

Topping:
¼ cup granulated sugar
½ teaspoon cinnamon
½ teaspoon processed cocoa
⅛ teaspoon ginger, ground
⅛ teaspoon cloves, ground

**Preparation**
1. Before cooking:
   a) Preheat the oven to 350°F;
   b) Grease two 9×5×3 loaf pans; and
   c) Line the bottoms of the pans with wax paper.
2. Cream the sugar by beating it with the butter.
3. Beat the eggs into the mixture one at a time.
4. Sift the flour, cocoa, cinnamon, salt, baking powder, and baking soda into a large bowl.
5. In another bowl, whisk together the water, buttermilk, and vanilla.
6. Make a well in the dry mixture and start pouring in the wet mixtures a little at a time, while whisking.
7. When the mixture starts becoming doughy, divide it in two and transfer it to the pans.
8. Mix together all the topping ingredients and sprinkle evenly on top of the mixture in both pans.
9. Bake for 50 to 60 minutes, or until the bread has set.

# Panera Bread's Cinnamon Crunch Bagel

This bagel can be prepared any time and eaten on the go or right before you leave the house. Have a restaurant-worthy breakfast right in your home!

*Serves: 8 – Preparation Time: 1 hour – Cooking Time: 25 minutes*
*Nutrition facts per serving: Calories 463, Total Fat 16 g, Carbs 71 g,*
*Protein 6 g, Sodium 296 mg*

**Ingredients**
Bread:
1¼ cups warm water, between 110 to 120°F
1 tablespoon yeast
1 tablespoon salt
4 tablespoons honey, divided

1½ cups whole wheat pastry flour
½ tablespoon cinnamon
1¾ cups bread flour
¾ cup white chocolate chips
Cornmeal, for sprinkling
4¼ quarts water

Topping:
¼ cup granulated sugar
¼ cup packed brown sugar
1 tablespoon cinnamon
⅓ cup coconut oil

**Preparation**
1. Activate the yeast by mixing it with the warm water and setting it aside for 10 minutes.
2. Add in 3 tablespoons of the honey, the salt, the pastry flour, and the cinnamon. Mix all the ingredients together with a dough mixer or wooden spoon. After a minute of mixing, or when the flour is fully incorporated, scrape the sides of the bowl and mix again for another few minutes.
3. Let the dough rest for 5 minutes—if lumps form, stir the batter to break them apart.
4. Add in half a cup of bread flour and start kneading. Keep adding the bread flour half a cup at a time until it is finished, while kneading the dough to distribute the flour throughout.
5. After about seven minutes of kneading, add in the white chocolate chips and continue kneading to completely incorporate the chips into the mixture.
6. Cover the bowl with a towel and leave the dough to rest for one hour.
7. After an hour, flour a flat surface where you can place your dough. Transfer the dough from its bowl to the floured surface and punch it down.

8. Cut the dough into 8 equal pieces. Roll them into ropes. Let the dough rest again, for 3 to 4 minutes.
9. Form a circle with each piece of dough, twisting the ends securely together. Sprinkle a baking sheet with cornmeal and place the dough circles on the sheet. Cover with a towel and let rest for 10 to 15 minutes.
10. While the dough is resting, prepare your materials by:
    (1) Bringing the water to a boil. When the water is boiling, add the remaining 1 tablespoon of honey. Keep the water at a low boil;
    (2) Preheat the oven to 450°F;
    (3) Line a baking sheet with parchment or wax paper; and
    (4) Mix the topping ingredients (except the oil) together.
11. After 15 minutes, place a few dough circles into the boiling water. Leave them to cook for 50 seconds on each side. When the bagels have boiled, transfer them to the baking sheet using a slotted spoon so as to drain off the water.
12. When all the bagels have boiled, brush each one with coconut oil and sprinkle with the sugar mixture.
13. Bake your bagels for 20 to 25 minutes, then transfer them to a wire rack to let them cool.

# Starbucks's Lemon Loaf

Lemon loaves are both refreshing and energizing. Have a slice of Starbucks-style lemon loaf before your day begins.

*Serves: 8 – Preparation Time: 15 minutes – Cooking Time: 45 minutes*
*Nutrition facts per serving: Calories 425.2, Total Fat 18.7 g, Carbs 60 g,*
*Protein 5 g, Sodium 310.8 mg*

## Ingredients

<u>Bread</u>:

1½ cups flour

½ teaspoon baking soda

½ teaspoon baking powder

½ teaspoon salt

1 cup sugar

3 eggs, room temperature

2 tablespoons butter, softened

1 teaspoon vanilla extract

⅓ cup lemon juice

½ cup oil

<u>Icing</u>:

1 cup + 1 tablespoon powdered sugar

2 tablespoons milk

½ teaspoon lemon extract

## Preparation

1. Get your baking materials ready by:
   a) Preheating your oven to 350°F;
   b) Greasing and flouring a 9×5×3 loaf pan; and
   c) Lining pan's bottom with wax paper.
2. Mix the first four ingredients in a large bowl—this is your dry mixture.
3. Beat the eggs, butter, vanilla, and lemon juice together in a medium bowl until the mixture becomes smooth. This is your wet mixture.
4. Make a well in the middle of the dry mixture and pour the wet mixture into the well.
5. Mix everything together with a whisk or your hand mixer. Add the oil. Do not stop mixing until everything is fully blended and smooth.

6. Pour the batter into the pan and bake it for 45 minutes—the bread is ready when you can stick a toothpick into it and it comes out clean.
7. While the bread is baking, make the icing by mixing the icing ingredients in a small bowl using a whisk or hand mixer until smooth.
8. When the bread is done baking, place it on a cooling rack and leave it for at least 20 minutes to cool.
9. When the bread is cool enough, pour the icing over the top. Wait for the icing to set before slicing.

# Waffle House's Waffle

There's nothing like a good waffle to kick-start your day. If you're craving for those to-die-for Waffle House waffles, here's a recipe that will satisfy those cravings.

*Serves: 6 – Preparation Time: 5 minutes – Cooking Time: 20 minutes*
*Nutrition facts per serving: Calories 313.8, Total Fat 12.4 g, Carbs 45 g,*
*Protein 5.9 g, Sodium 567.9 mg*

## *Ingredients*
1½ cups all-purpose flour
1 teaspoon salt
½ teaspoon baking soda
1 egg
½ cup + 1 tablespoon granulated white sugar
2 tablespoons butter, softened
2 tablespoons shortening
½ cup half-and-half

½ cup milk

¼ cup buttermilk

¼ teaspoon vanilla

## Preparation

1. Prepare the dry mixture by sifting the flour into a bowl and mixing it with the salt and baking soda.
2. In a medium bowl, lightly beat an egg. When the egg has become frothy, beat in the butter, sugar, and shortening. When the mixture is thoroughly mixed, beat in the half-and-half, vanilla, milk, and buttermilk. Continue beating the mixture until it is smooth.
3. While beating the wet mixture, slowly pour in the dry mixture, making sure to mix thoroughly and remove all the lumps.
4. Chill the batter overnight (optional, but recommended; if you can't chill the mixture overnight, leave it for at least 15 to 20 minutes).
5. Take the batter out of the refrigerator. Preheat and grease your waffle iron.
6. Cook each waffle for three to four minutes. Serve with butter and syrup.

# Mimi's Café Santa Fé Omelet

Here's another egg recipe to kick-start your morning. Have a plate of this scrambled omelet to get your day off to a good start.

*Serves: 1 – Preparation Time: 10 minutes – Cooking Time: 10 minutes*
*Nutrition facts per serving: Calories 519, Total Fat 32 g, Carbs 60 g,*
*Protein 14 g, Sodium 463 mg*

## *Ingredients*
Chipotle Sauce:
1 cup marinara or tomato sauce
¾ cup water
½ cup chipotle in adobo sauce
1 teaspoon kosher salt

Omelet:
1 tablespoon onions, diced
1 tablespoon jalapeños, diced
2 tablespoons cilantro, chopped
2 tablespoons tomatoes, diced
¼ cup fried corn tortillas, cut into strips
3 eggs, beaten

2 slices cheese

1 dash of salt and pepper

Garnish:

2 ounces chipotle sauce, hot

¼ cup fried corn tortillas, cut into strips

1 tablespoon sliced green onions

1 tablespoon guacamole

**Preparation**

1. Melt some butter in a pan over medium heat, making sure to coat the entire pan.
2. Sauté the jalapeños, cilantro, tomatoes, onions, and tortilla strips for about a minute.
3. Add the eggs, seasoning them with salt and pepper and stirring occasionally.
4. Flip the omelet when it has set. Place the cheese on the top half.
5. When the cheese starts to become melty, fold the omelet in half and transfer to a plate.
6. Garnish the omelet with chipotle sauce, guacamole, green onions, and corn tortillas.

# Copycat Snack and Side Recipes

## Taco Bell's Double Decker Tacos

Tacos are a marvelous snack. Have a Taco Bell Double Decker Taco to satisfy your cravings.

*Serves: 10 – Preparation Time: 30 minutes – Cooking Time: 15 minutes*
*Nutrition facts per serving: Calories 485, Total Fat 26.3 g, Carbs 37.3 g, Protein 18.9 g, Sodium 741 mg*

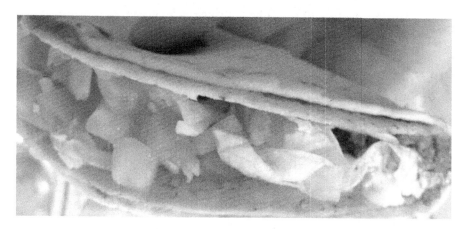

### Ingredients
Taco:
1 pound ground beef
1 ounce taco seasoning mix, divided
1 can (16 ounces) refried beans
⅔ cup water
12 crisp taco shells
Sour cream for serving

Guacamole:
2 avocados
2 tablespoons diced onions
1 fresh lime, juiced
Salt and black pepper to taste

<u>Assembling:</u>
12 soft flour tortillas, about 7-inch diameter
2 cups shredded cheddar cheese
1 cup shredded lettuce
1 large tomato, chopped
¼ red onion, chopped
½ cup sour cream
Salt and black pepper to taste

### *Preparation*
1. Preheat the oven to 350°F.
2. Cook the beef for 10 to 15 minutes over medium heat, sprinkling it with ¾ ounce of the taco seasoning. When the beef is brown and crumbly, remove it from the heat and set aside.
3. Season the refried beans with the remaining taco seasoning mix by placing the beans, water, and seasoning in a small pot and mixing and mashing everything together. Mash the beans and bring the mixture to a simmer.
4. Heat the taco shells in the oven for 3 to 5 minutes.
5. While the taco shells are being heated, make the guacamole by mashing all the guacamole ingredients together.
6. To assemble the tacos, start by covering one side of each flour tortilla with 2 tablespoons of bean mixture and wrapping the flour tortilla around a taco shell. Then place the following by layers inside the taco shell
   a) 2 tablespoons beef
   b) 2 tablespoons cheese
   c) Shredded lettuce
   d) Chopped tomato and onion
   Serve with guacamole and sour cream on the side

# Domino's Stuffed Bread

Domino's is famous not just for their pizza, but also for their stuffed bread. It's a perfect combination of crispy and chewy that will satisfy all your guests.

*Serves: 6 – Preparation Time: 10 minutes – Cooking Time: 25 minutes*
*Nutrition facts per serving: Calories 420, Total Fat 26.5 g, Carbs 25.7 g,*
*Protein 19.4 g, Sodium 810 mg*

## *Ingredients*
1 package (11 ounces) French bread dough, refrigerated
4 tablespoons melted butter, divided
1 tablespoon cornmeal
1 cup shredded mozzarella cheese
1 cup shredded Mexican cheese blend
1 cup + 1 tablespoon shredded cheddar cheese, divided
1 tablespoon freshly grated parmesan cheese
1 pinch dried parsley

1 pinch garlic powder

Cooking spray

## *Preparation*

1. Before cooking, preheat the oven to 350°F and grease a large baking sheet with cooking spray.
2. Choose a flat work surface and roll out your dough into a rectangle.
3. Brush one side of the dough rectangle with 3 tablespoons of the melted butter and the cornmeal. Flip the dough over and cover the other side with the mozzarella, Mexican cheese, and 1 cup of the cheddar cheese.
4. Seal the stuffing in by folding the dough in half and pressing the edges of the dough together with your fingers.
5. Brush the remaining melted butter all over the dough and sprinkle it with the parmesan, the remaining cheddar cheese, the parsley, and the onion and garlic powders.
6. Score the dough with 1-inch-deep lines to make it easier to separate after baking.
7. Bake the dough for 25 minutes. Let it cool for 5 minutes before serving.

# Red Lobster's Cheddar Bay Biscuit

You can make these biscuits in just under 40 minutes – and your guests and family will thank you for it!

*Serves: 9 – Preparation Time: 15 minutes – Cooking Time: 25 minutes*
*Nutrition facts per serving: Calories 160, Total Fat 10 g, Carbs 3 g,*
*Protein 16 g, Sodium 380 mg*

## Ingredients
Biscuit:
2½ cups Bisquick biscuit mix
4 tablespoons **cold** butter
1 cup sharp cheddar cheese, grated

¾ cup cold whole milk
¼ teaspoon garlic powder

Garlic Butter Glaze:
2 tablespoons butter, melted
½ teaspoon garlic powder
¼ teaspoon dried parsley flakes
1 pinch salt

## Preparation

1. Prepare your materials by:
   a) Preheating your oven to 450°F; and
   b) Greasing a cookie sheet.
2. Lightly mix the biscuit mix and the butter so that they are combined, but small chunks remain.
3. Mix in the cheddar cheese, garlic powder and milk by hand.
4. When the ingredients are evenly distributed, scoop 9 equal portions of the mixture onto the cookie sheet.
5. Bake the biscuits for 15 to 17 minutes, or until the tops turn light brown.
6. While the biscuits are baking, prepare the glaze by mixing all the glaze ingredients together in a small bowl.
7. When the biscuits are done, transfer them to a cooling rack and brush the garlic butter glaze over the tops before serving.

# KFC's Buttermilk Biscuits

Here's another well-loved biscuit recipe. It takes just a little over 20 minutes, but many people can attest to its deliciousness.

*Serves: 15 – Preparation Time: 7 minutes – Cooking Time: 15 minutes*
*Nutrition facts per serving: Calories 254.7, Total Fat 13.1 g, Carbs 29.7 g,*
*Protein 4.3 g, Sodium 659.3 mg*

## Ingredients
½ cup butter
2 tablespoons + 1½ teaspoons sugar, divided
1 egg, beaten
¾ cup buttermilk
¼ cup club soda
1 teaspoon salt
5 cups Bisquick biscuit mix

## *Preparation*

1. Preheat the oven to 450°F.
2. Mix all the ingredients together to make a dough.
3. Flour a flat surface, place the dough on the surface, and roll it until it is ¾ of an inch thick.
4. Cut the dough and shape the pieces into biscuits.
5. Place the cut dough onto a baking sheet and bake for 12 to 15 minutes.

# Taco Bell's Enchiritos

Simple yet delicious. If you're craving for a sauce-covered taco, this recipe is perfect for you.

*Serves: 12 – Preparation Time: 20 minutes – Cooking Time: 15 minutes*
*Nutrition facts per serving: Calories 310, Total Fat 16 g, Carbs 27 g,*
*Protein 15 g, Sodium 1260 mg*

## *Ingredients*
<u>Seasoning</u>
¼ cup all-purpose flour
1 tablespoon chili powder
1 teaspoon salt
½ teaspoon dried onion flakes
½ teaspoon paprika
¼ teaspoon onion powder
1 dash garlic powder

Tortillas
1 pound lean ground beef
½ cup water
1 16-ounce can refried beans
12 small flour tortillas
½ cup onion, diced
116-ounce can red chili sauce
2 cups cheddar cheese, shredded
Some green onions, for serving
Some sour cream, for serving

## Preparation

1. Mix all the seasoning ingredients together, and then coat the beef in the seasoning using your hands. Make sure that the beef fully absorbs the flavor from the spices.
2. Brown the seasoned beef in the water over medium heat, for 8 to 10 minutes. Stir the beef occasionally to remove lumps.
3. While the beef is browning, microwave the beans on high for 2 minutes.
4. Wrap the tortillas in a wet towel and microwave for 1 minute.
5. When the beef is done, assemble the tortillas:
   a) Place some beans in the middle of the tortilla;
   b) Place some beef on top, add some onion;
   c) Roll up the tortilla by bringing both ends together in the center;
   d) Place the tortilla in a microwave-safe casserole; and
   e) Spread the chili sauce and cheddar cheese on top of the tortilla.
6. Repeat step 5 until casserole is full.
7. Heat the entire dish in the microwave for 2-3 minutes. The dish is done when the cheese melts.
8. Serve with green onions and sour cream, if desired.

# Applebee's Spicy Queso Blanco

If you're planning to serve chips at your next get-together, then here is a dip recipe that will make you famous with the guests. It tastes just like Applebee's!

*Makes about 1 ¼ cups – Preparation Time: 10 min. – Cooking Time: 5 min.*
*Nutrition facts per serving: Calories 1049, Total Fat 62 g, Carbs 99 g,*
*Protein 25 g, Sodium 2510 mg*

### Ingredients
Queso Blanco:
1 tablespoon vegetable oil
½ small onion, minced
1-3 jalapeño peppers, seeded, deveined, minced
½ cup heavy cream

8 ounces Monterey Jack cheese, cut into chunks
4 ounces white American cheese, cut into chunks
1 tablespoon cilantro, chopped
Some cooking oil

Pico de Gallo:
½ small onion, chopped
½ tablespoon fresh cilantro, chopped
1 jalapeño peppers, seeded, deveined, minced
1 Roma tomato, de-seeded; diced

**Preparation**
1. Heat the oil over medium heat, then sauté the onion and jalapeños for 3 to 5 minutes.
2. Add the heavy cream to the mixture and bring it to a simmer.
3. Slowly add in the cheese, making sure that all the chunks melt completely before adding more.
4. When all the cheese is melted, mix in the cilantro. When the mixture is cooked, transfer it into a small bowl—this is your Queso Blanco.
5. Make a simple Pico de Gallo by mixing all the Pico de Gallo ingredients together in a medium-sized bowl.
6. Top the Queso Blanco with some Pico de Gallo before serving.

# Red Lobster's White Cheddar Mashed Potato

A mouthful of this creamy, cheesy mashed potato will have you asking for more. Bring Red Lobster's famous side dish to your home.

*Serves: 4 – Preparation Time: 5 minutes – Cooking Time: 10 minutes*
*Nutrition facts per serving: Calories 490.7, Total Fat 31.4 g, Carbs 41.4 g, Protein 12.7 g, Sodium 787.8 mg*

### Ingredients
2 pounds potatoes, peeled, quartered
2 ounces unsalted butter, at room temperature
⅓ cup heavy cream
¼ cup sour cream
4 ounces white cheddar cheese, grated
1 teaspoon salt
½ teaspoon white pepper

## Preparation

1. Bring some water to a boil in a pot, then place the potatoes inside.
2. Keep the potatoes boiling until they are soft enough to mash with a fork.
3. When the potatoes are tender enough, transfer them to a large bowl and mash them with a fork, potato masher, or electric mixer.
4. When no more chunks remain, add the butter and continue to mash until the butter gets mixed evenly into the potatoes.
5. Add the heavy cream and do the same.
6. Add the sour cream and continue mixing.
7. Slowly add in the cheese, mixing it thoroughly with the mashed potatoes.
8. Season the potatoes with salt and pepper and serve.

# T.G.I. Friday's Fried Green Beans

This healthy snack has both flavor and nutrients. Add that extra crunch to your meal in a healthy way.

*Serves: 4 – Preparation Time: 5 minutes – Cooking Time: 35 minutes*
*Nutrition facts per serving: Calories 441.2, Total Fat 20.8 g, Carbs 52 g,*
*Protein 11.7 g, Sodium 1093.5 mg*

**Ingredients**

Green Beans:

4 cups vegetable or chicken broth

6–8 ounces fresh green beans

1 egg, beaten

1 cup milk

1 cup flour

1 cup plain or seasoned dry breadcrumbs

¾ teaspoon salt

¼ teaspoon onion powder

⅛ teaspoon garlic powder

Vegetable oil or shortening for frying

Wasabi Cucumber Ranch Dip:

½ cup bottled ranch dressing

½ cup cucumber. peeled, seeded, minced

1 tablespoon milk

1½ teaspoons prepared horseradish

1 teaspoon apple cider vinegar

1 teaspoon wasabi powder

⅛ teaspoon salt

1 pinch cayenne pepper

## Preparation

1. Place the dip ingredients in your blender and blend everything until smooth.
2. Transfer the mixture to a bowl and place in the refrigerator.
3. Place the broth and green beans in a pot and boil for 15 minutes.
4. While the green beans are cooking, take three shallow bowls for dipping. In one bowl, beat the egg and milk. In another, place the flour. In the third, mix together the breadcrumbs, salt, and onion and garlic powder.
5. Remove the beans from the pot and shock in cold water.
6. Shake the beans dry and transfer them to a dry bowl.
7. One by one, dip the beans into the flour, then egg mixture, then breadcrumbs. Make sure to completely coat each bean.
8. Place enough oil in a pan to cover the beans. Place the oil over fire and heat to 350°F.
9. Fry the beans until golden brown, and then transfer to a plate covered with a paper towel.
10. When all the beans are cooked, place the beans and the dip on a plate and serve.

# Cracker Barrel's Hash Brown Casserole

If the last potato dish wasn't quite what you were looking for, here is a hash brown recipe just like Cracker Barrel's. Have it for breakfast, lunch, dinner, or a snack.

*Serves: 10 – Preparation Time: 15 minutes – Cooking Time: 45 minutes*
*Nutrition facts per serving: Calories 376.3, Total Fat 21.1 g, Carbs 37.2 g,*
*Protein 9.7 g, Sodium 674.3 mg*

## Ingredients

1 tablespoon butter or margarine, melted
1 cup milk
½ cup beef broth
1 teaspoon garlic salt or regular salt
¼ teaspoon black pepper
¼ cup onions, minced or finely diced
26–30 ounces hash browns, shredded
2 cups shredded cheddar cheese, divided

## Preparation

1. Preheat your oven to 425°F and grease a 9×13 baking pan.
2. In a bowl, thoroughly mix together the first 5 ingredients. Set aside.
3. Place the hash browns and diced onions in a skillet, with half of the shredded cheese in the middle. Place the skillet over medium heat, and when the cheese starts to melt, start folding the mixture.
4. Place the heated hash browns in the baking pan and pour the liquid mixture over them.
5. Mix the milk and broth mixture and the hash browns until the hash browns absorb the liquid.
6. Even out the surface of the hash browns by smoothening it with a spoon. Cover with foil and place in the oven. Bake for 30 minutes. Remove foil and add remaining cheese. Bake for another 10-15 minutes until the cheese is melted and golden brown. Let cool for about 10 minutes before serving.

# Tony Roma's Onion Loaf

Tony Roma's serves onion rings as a loaf—and everyone loves it. If you want to make some at home, here's how.

*Serves: 6 – Preparation Time: 30 minutes – Cooking Time: 15 minutes*
*Nutrition facts per serving: Calories 800, Total Fat 12 g, Carbs 114 g,*
*Protein 11 g, Sodium 1329 mg*

### Ingredients

4 to 6 white onions
1 cup milk
3 eggs, beaten
Salt to taste
2 cups Bisquick or dry pancake mix
Oil

Garnish:
Parsley

### Preparation

1. Slice the onions in half and separate the rings.
2. Mix the milk, eggs, and salt in one bowl, and the place the Bisquick in another.
3. Place the individual onion rings into the egg mixture and let sit for 30 minutes.
4. When the onion rings are almost done soaking, heat up some oil to 375°F.
5. Place the onion rings into the hot oil one by one and cook until they are golden brown.
6. Place the onion rings into an 8×4 loaf pan while they are still hot to pack them together—take note: do not press; just let the oil do its work.
7. When the onion rings have set, place the loaf on a plate and sprinkle it with parsley.

# Romano's Macaroni Grill Rosemary Bread

Bread is always a great snack. This aromatic loaf will get your blood pumping whatever time of day you choose to consume it.

*Serves: 2 loaves – Preparation Time: 1 hour 10 min. – Cooking Time: 20 min.*
*Nutrition facts per serving: Calories 716.7, Total Fat 13.6 g, Carbs 128.4 g,*
*Protein 18.7 g, Sodium 1274.4 mg*

## Ingredients
Some olive oil
1 tablespoon instant yeast
1 tablespoon sugar
1 cup warm water
2½ cups bread flour
1 teaspoon salt
1 tablespoon butter
2 tablespoons rosemary, divided

## Preparation

1. To get started:
   a) Grease a bowl with olive oil;
   b) Grease a baking pan or cookie sheet; and
   c) Preheat the oven to 375°F.
2. Place the yeast, sugar and water in a food processor or bowl and leave to rest.
3. When the yeast mixture starts bubbling, add in the rest of the ingredients, reserving 1 tablespoon of rosemary, and mix.
4. Knead the dough by hand or with the food processor for 5 to 10 minutes.
5. When the dough becomes elastic and smooth, place it in the greased bowl and cover the bowl with a towel. Let the dough rest for 1 hour.
6. When the dough has doubled in size, flatten it by punching it down. Then halve it.
7. Place the two halves in two separate bowls and set aside for another 10 minutes. After the dough has rested for 10 minutes, shape it into ovals.
8. Top the dough with the remaining rosemary, pressing it so that it gets stuck to the dough.
9. Let the dough rest for another 45 minutes.
10. After the dough has rested for the last time, place the two halves in the oven and bake for 15 to 20 minutes.
11. Remove the bread from the oven and allow to cool before serving.

# Cheesecake Factory's Chicken Pot Stickers

This is a good recipe whether you have guests over or just want to have a little snack. These chicken pot stickers taste just like Cheesecake Factory's special dish.

*Yields 48 – Preparation Time: 15 minutes – Cooking Time: 45 minutes*
*Nutrition facts per pot sticker: Calories 75, Total Fat 2 g, Carbs 18 g,*
*Protein 4 g, Sodium 462 mg*

### Ingredients

<u>Filling</u>
1½ pounds ground chicken
½ cup red bell pepper, finely chopped
½ cup green cabbage, shredded
⅓ cup chopped green onions
2 teaspoons chopped ginger root
1 teaspoon sesame oil
¼ teaspoon white pepper

<u>Other ingredients</u>
1 egg white
1 cup water
1 package (10 ounces) round wonton skins
4 cups chicken broth, divided
4 teaspoons reduced-sodium soy sauce, divided

<u>Dipping sauce</u>
1 chicken broth
¼ cup soy sauce

<u>Garnish</u>
Green onions or chive, finely chiseled
Nori thin strips (optional)

### Preparation

1. To make the filling, mix the filling ingredients together, thoroughly incorporating each ingredient into the mixture.
2. Brush each of the wonton skins with water.
3. Place 1 tablespoon of the stuffing mixture at the center of the wonton skin and create 5 pleats on one side of the wrapper.
4. Fold the wrapper over, sealing the mixture inside.
5. Repeat steps 3 and 4 until you are out of filling.

6. Grease a large pan and cook pot stickers in batches over medium heat until they turn light brown. Do not overcrowd the pan.
7. Increase heat to medium-high. Pour 1 cup of the chicken broth and 1 teaspoon of soy sauce over the cooking pot stickers. Cover the pan and let the mixture sit until all the liquid has evaporated. Transfer pot stickers in a plate and cover with foil to keep warm.
8. Repeat steps 6 and 7 for the remaining pot stickers.
9. To make the dipping sauce, use the same pan. Add 1 cup chicken broth and ¼ cup soy sauce and bring to a boil on high heat. Scrap the pan's bottom to release all bits of flavor. Reduce heat to medium and let simmer until the sauce has reduce by half, about 3-5 minutes.
10. To serve, divide pot stickers between serving plates add some of the dipping sauce to the serving plate, top with pot stickers and garnish with green onions or chives, and nori thin strips, if desired.

# P.F. Chang's Chef John's Chicken Lettuce Wraps

If you are in the mood for a healthier snack, here's P.F. Chang's chicken lettuce wraps. It's filling and tasty!

*Serves: 8 – Preparation Time: 35 minutes – Cooking Time: 15 minutes*
*Nutrition facts per serving: Calories 212, Total Fat 10.7 g, Carbs 10.8 g,*
*Protein 17.6 g, Sodium 332 mg*

### Ingredients

<u>Chicken Mix:</u>
1½ pounds skinless, boneless chicken thighs, coarsely chopped
1 can (8 ounces) water chestnuts, drained, minced
1 cup shiitake mushroom caps, diced
½ cup yellow onion, minced
⅓ cup green onion, chopped
1 tablespoon soy sauce
1 tablespoon ginger, freshly grated
2 teaspoons brown sugar
2 tablespoons vegetable oil

<u>Glaze:</u>
¼ cup chicken stock
¼ cup rice wine vinegar
4 cloves garlic, minced
1 tablespoon ketchup
1 tablespoon soy sauce
2 teaspoons sesame oil
2 teaspoons brown sugar
½ teaspoon red pepper flakes
½ teaspoon dry mustard

<u>Herbs and Wrap:</u>
1½ tablespoons fresh cilantro, chopped
1½ tablespoons fresh basil, chopped
1½ tablespoons green onion, chopped
16 leaves iceberg lettuce, or as needed

### Preparation

1. Mix all the chicken mix ingredients (except the oil) together in a bowl. Cover the bowl with plastic wrap and place in the refrigerator.
2. Whisk all the glaze ingredients together until everything is mixed thoroughly.

51

3. When the glaze is ready, cook the chicken mix ingredients in the oil over high heat.
4. After 2 minutes, when the chicken is cooked, pour half of the glaze over the chicken mix. Continue cooking the entire mixture until the glaze caramelizes. This should take 10 to 15 minutes.
5. Reduce the heat to medium to low, then add the remaining glaze to the mixture. Cook for around 3 more minutes, constantly stirring.
6. Stir in the chopped herbs (i.e. cilantro, basil, and onion) and continue cooking until they are incorporated into the chicken mixture.
7. Transfer the chicken to a plate and serve with lettuce.

# Copycat Soup Recipes

## Outback's French Onion Soup

This decadent French onion soup is easy to make and can make a meal on its own. If you have a special love for Outback's special dishes, here's one that you can make for dinner.

*Serves: 4 – Preparation Time: 15 minutes – Cooking Time: 50 minutes*
*Nutrition facts per serving: Calories 420, Total Fat 29 g, Carbs 21 g,*
*Protein 19 g, Sodium 2120 mg*

### Ingredients:
2 cups sweet yellow onion, quartered and sliced
½ cup sweet cream butter
½ teaspoon salt
1 tablespoon flour
4 cups beef stock
1 tablespoon fresh thyme

1 teaspoon coarse ground black pepper
4 baguette slices, approximately ½-inch thick
8 slices Provolone cheese

## Directions:

1. Melt the butter in a stock pot over medium heat.
2. Add the onions and salt, and sauté for 3 minutes or until translucent but not browned. Add the flour and stir.
3. Add the beef stock, increase the heat to medium-high, and bring to a boil. Let boil for 1 minute.
4. Reduce the heat to low, season with thyme and black pepper. Cover and let simmer for 25-30 minutes.
5. While the soup is simmering, toast the baguette slices to a medium golden brown. Make sure each slice will fit comfortably in your soup bowl.
6. Preheat the broiler.
7. When the soup is done simmering, ladle it into oven proof serving bowls.
8. Top each bowl with a toasted baguette slice and 2 slices of Provolone cheese. Place under the broiler for 1-2 minutes, or until the cheese is well melted and lightly caramelized.
9. Remove from the broiler carefully and serve immediately.

# T.G.I. Friday's Black Bean Soup

This soup is perfect for a cold, dreary day. If you're in the mood for T.G.I. Friday's black bean soup, then here is a recipe that you can make right at home.

*Serves: 6 – Preparation Time: 10 minutes – Cooking Time: 1 hour 15 minutes*
*Nutrition facts per serving: Calories 392.5, Total Fat 7.8 g, Carbs 59.3 g,*
*Protein 23 g, Sodium 458.9 mg*

## Ingredients

2 tablespoons vegetable oil

¾ cup white onion, diced

¾ cup celery, diced

½ cup carrot, diced

¼ cup green bell pepper, diced

2 tablespoons garlic, minced

4 15-ounce cans black beans, rinsed

4 cups chicken stock

2 tablespoons apple cider vinegar

2 teaspoons chili powder

½ teaspoon cayenne pepper

½ teaspoon cumin

½ teaspoon salt

¼ teaspoon hickory liquid smoke

## Preparation

1. In a pan, sauté the onion, celery, carrot, bell pepper, and garlic in the heated oil for 15 minutes over low heat. Make sure to keep the vegetables from burning.
2. While the vegetables are cooking, strain and wash the black beans.
3. Add 3 cups of the washed beans and a cup of chicken stock to a food processor and purée until smooth.
4. When the onion mixture is cooked, add the rest of the ingredients (including the bean purée) to the pan.
5. Bring everything to a boil, then lower the heat and allow the mixture to simmer for another 50 to 60 minutes.
6. Transfer the soup to bowls and serve.

# Olive Garden's Minestrone Soup

Minestrone soup is a classic. Here is Olive Garden's take on this famous dish.

*Serves: 8 – Preparation Time: 5 minutes – Cooking Time: 40 minutes*
*Nutrition facts per serving: Calories 353.5, Total Fat 6.3 g, Carbs 57.8 g,*
*Protein 19.2 g, Sodium 471.7 mg*

### *Ingredients*
3 tablespoons olive oil
½ cup green beans, sliced
¼ cup celery, diced
1 cup white onion diced)
1 zucchini, diced
4 teaspoons minced garlic
4 cups vegetable broth
1 can (15 ounces each) red kidney beans, drained
2 cans (15 ounces each) small white beans, drained

1 can (14 ounce) tomatoes, diced
1 carrot, peeled and diced
2 tablespoons fresh Italian parsley, chopped finely
1½ teaspoons dried oregano
1½ teaspoons salt
½ teaspoon ground black pepper
½ teaspoon dried basil
¼ teaspoon dried thyme
3 cups hot water
4 cups fresh baby spinach
½ cup small shell pasta
Shredded parmesan cheese for serving

## *Preparation*

1. Chop and mince the ingredients as specified.
2. Sauté the green beans, celery, onion, zucchini, and garlic in olive oil in a soup pot until the onions become translucent.
3. Add in the rest of the ingredients, except the beans, pasta, and spinach leaves, and bring the mixture to a boil.
4. When the mixture is boiling, add in the beans, spinach and pasta. Reduce the heat and allow to simmer for another 20 minutes.
5. Ladle into a bowl, sprinkle with parmesan if desired, and serve.

# Panera Bread's Vegetarian Summer Corn Chowder

Have some bread with this delicious soup for dinner during a cold, rainy night. It's definitely comforting and warm.

*Serves: 6 – Preparation Time: 10 minutes – Cooking Time: 45 minutes*
*Nutrition facts per serving: Calories 320, Total Fat 20 g, Carbs 34 g,*
*Protein 5 g, Sodium 1310 mg*

## *Ingredients*
2 tablespoons olive oil
1 tablespoon unsalted butter
1 medium red onion, diced
3 tablespoons all-purpose flour
2 russet potatoes, diced
5 cups unsalted vegetable stock
½ cup red bell pepper, diced
½ cup green bell pepper, diced

4 cups whole corn kernels
¼ teaspoon black pepper, ground
1 cup half-and-half cream
Salt and pepper to taste
Chives, thinly sliced, for garnish
Bacon bits, for garnish

## *Preparation*

1. Sauté the onion in butter and oil over low heat. When the onion becomes translucent, add in the flour and cook for another 5 minutes.
2. Dice the potatoes into quarter-inch cubes and add it to the simmering mixture. Add the broth, then turn the heat up and bring the mixture to a boil.
3. Reduce the heat to medium and continue simmering for 15 minutes.
4. Dice the bell peppers into quarter-inch cubes and add them to the mixture. Also add in the corn, pepper, cream, salt, and pepper, and allow the mixture to simmer for another 15 minutes.
5. Transfer the soup into a bowl and garnish with chives and bacon, if desired.

# Red Lobster's Clam Chowder

This recipe gets Red Lobster's seafood chowder soup just right. Enjoy this creamy soup whenever you're in the mood for it.

*Serves: 8 – Preparation Time: 20 minutes – Cooking Time: 30 minutes*
*Nutrition facts per serving: Calories 436.1, Total Fat 26.5 g, Carbs 30.1 g,*
*Protein 20.3 g, Sodium 1987 mg*

## Ingredients
2 tablespoons butter
1 cup onion, diced
½ cup leek, white part, thinly sliced
¼ teaspoon garlic, minced
½ cup celery, diced
2 tablespoons flour
4 cups milk
1 cup clams with juice, diced
1 cup potato, diced

1 tablespoon salt
¼ teaspoon white pepper
1 teaspoon dried thyme
½ cup heavy cream
Saltine crackers for serving

## *Preparation*

1. In a pot, sauté the onion, leek, garlic, and celery in butter over medium heat.
2. After 3 minutes, remove the vegetables from the heat and add the flour.
3. Whisk in the milk and clam juice.
4. Return the mixture to the heat and bring it to a boil.
5. Add the potatoes, salt, pepper, and thyme, then lower the heat to let the mixture simmer. Continue mixing for another 10 minutes while the soup is simmering.
6. Add in the clams and let the mixture simmer for 5 to 8 minutes, or until the clams are cooked.
7. Add the heavy cream and cook for a few more minutes.
8. Transfer the soup to a bowl and serve with saltine crackers.

# Carrabba's Mama Mandola Sicilian Chicken Soup

Have you tried Carrabba's chicken soup? It's an amazing mix of heartiness and creaminess that will just send your taste buds to heaven.

*Serves: 10 – Preparation Time: 15 minutes – Cooking Time: 8 hours*
*Nutrition facts per serving: Calories 320, Total Fat 0 g, Carbs 57 g,*
*Protein 13 g, Sodium 525.3 mg*

## Ingredients
4 carrots, peeled, diced
4 stalks celery, diced
1 green bell pepper, cored, diced
2 medium white potatoes, diced
1 white onion, diced
3 cloves garlic, minced

1 can (14.5 ounces) tomatoes, diced, with juice
1 tablespoon fresh parsley
1 teaspoon Italian seasoning
½ teaspoon white pepper
Dash of crushed red pepper flakes, to taste
2 boneless skinless chicken breasts, shredded
2 32-ounces containers chicken stock
1 ½ teaspoons salt
1 pound Ditalini pasta

### Preparation

1. Dice and chop the vegetables as instructed.
2. Place them in a slow cooker and sprinkle with the parsley, seasoning, and white and red pepper. Mix everything together.
3. Add the shredded chicken and stock and mix again.
4. Cover the mixture and cook it for 8 hours on low heat.
5. When the soup is almost ready, bring a salt-and-water mixture to a boil to cook the pasta.
6. Add the cooked pasta to the soup and continue cooking for 5 minutes and serve.

# Carrabba's Sausage and Lentil Soup

If you like Carrabba's soups, then here is another one. Bring Carrabba's well-loved sausage and lentil soup to your dinner table.

*Serves: 6 – Preparation Time: 10 minutes – Cooking Time: 1 hour 5 minutes*
*Nutrition facts per serving: Calories 221, Total Fat 10 g, Carbs 20 g,*
*Protein 13 g, Sodium 1182 mg*

### Ingredients
1 pound Italian sausages
1 large onion, diced
1 stalk celery, diced
2 large carrots, diced
1 small zucchini, diced
6 cups low sodium chicken broth

2 cans (14.5 ounces each) tomatoes, diced, with juice
2 cups dry lentils
2–3 garlic cloves, minced
1 ½ teaspoons salt
1 teaspoon black pepper
1-3 pinches red pepper flakes, more if you like it spicier
1 teaspoon dry basil
½ teaspoon dry oregano
½ teaspoon parsley
½ teaspoon dry thyme
Parmesan cheese for garnishing

### Preparation

1. Preheat the oven to 350°F. Place sausages on a baking dish and poke a few holes in each sausage with a fork. Bake for 20-30 minutes, or until the sausages are done. Let cool down and slice the sausages.
2. Chop and mince the ingredients as specified in the ingredients list.
3. Place all the ingredients, except the parmesan cheese, in a large pot..
4. Bring the soup to a boil, then lower the heat and cover the pot.
5. Let the mixture simmer for an hour, adding water to reduce thickness when necessary. If you want a thicker soup, puree a portion of the soup and return it.
6. Ladle the soup into bowls and garnish with parmesan cheese before serving.

# Denny's Vegetable and Beef Barley Soup

If you're looking for a beefy, rich soup, then here is one that will satisfy your cravings. This dish will definitely whet your appetite.

*Serves: 4 – Preparation Time: 10 minutes – Cooking Time: 40 minutes*
*Nutrition facts per serving: Calories 244.5, Total Fat 11.4 g, Carbs 17.1 g,*
*Protein 20 g, Sodium 1818.2 mg*

## Ingredients
½ pound ground beef
16 ounces frozen mixed vegetables
1 can (14.5 ounces) tomatoes, diced, with juice
¼ cup barley
32-ounce beef broth
Salt and pepper

### Preparation

1. Place the ground beef in a pot and cook until brown.
2. Add in the vegetables, tomatoes, barley, and broth, and bring the entire mixture to a simmer.
3. Add salt and pepper for seasoning and leave the mixture to simmer for at least 40 minutes.
4. Ladle the soup into bowls and serve. The longer you leave the soup to simmer, the better it will taste.

# Outback's Walkabout Soup

Don't miss out on this creamy goodness just because you don't want to leave the house. Here is a recipe that tastes just like Outback's special soup.

*Serves: 4 – Preparation Time: 10 minutes – Cooking Time: 45 minutes*
*Nutrition facts per serving: Calories 329, Total Fat 25 g, Carbs 17 g,*
*Protein 6 g, Sodium 1061 mg*

**Ingredients**
Thick white Sauce:
3 tablespoons butter
3 tablespoons flour
¼ teaspoon salt
1½ cups whole milk

Soup:
2 cups yellow sweet onions, thinly sliced
3 tablespoons butter
1 can (14.5 ounces) chicken broth

½ teaspoon salt
¼ teaspoon fresh ground black pepper
2 chicken bouillon cubes
¼ cup Velveeta cubes, diced, packed
1½–1¾ cups white sauce (recipe above)
Cheddar cheese for garnish, shredded
Crusty bread for serving

### Preparation

1. Make the thick white sauce first. Make a roux by cooking melted butter and flour over medium heat. Slowly pour the milk onto the roux, a little at a time, while constantly stirring the mixture. When the mixture reaches a pudding-like consistency, remove it from heat and set aside.
2. In a soup pot, sauté the onions in the butter over medium heat until they become translucent.
3. Add the rest of the ingredients, except the cheese and white sauce, to the pot and mix everything together.
4. When the mixture has heated up completely, add the cheese and white sauce. Bring the entire mixture to a simmer on medium-low heat. Continuously stir the soup until everything is completely mixed together.
5. When the cheese has melted, turn the heat lower and continue to cook the soup for another 30 to 45 minutes.
6. Ladle the soup into bowls and garnish with cheese. Serve with a side of bread.

# Disneyland's Monterey Clam Chowder

Prepare a magical dish from the most magical place on earth. This clam chowder soup will definitely take your taste buds on the ride of their lives.

*Serves: 4 – Preparation Time: 15 minutes – Cooking Time: 1 hour*
*Nutrition facts per serving: Calories 472.3, Total Fat 36.9 g, Carbs 27.4 g, Protein 9.3 g, Sodium 771.5 mg*

### Ingredients
5 tablespoons butter
5 tablespoons flour
2 tablespoons vegetable oil
1½ cups potatoes (peeled, diced)
½ cup onion, diced
½ cup red pepper
½ cup green pepper
½ cup celery
2¼ cups clam juice

1½ cups heavy cream
1 cup clams, chopped
1 tablespoon fresh thyme or ½ tablespoon dried thyme
¼–½ teaspoon salt
1 pinch white pepper
⅓–½ teaspoon Tabasco sauce
4 individual sourdough round breads made into bowls
Chives for garnish (optional)

## Preparation

1. Make a roux by mixing melted butter and flour over medium heat for 10 minutes. Flour burns quickly, so make sure to watch the mixture closely. Set the roux aside.
2. Sauté the potatoes, onions, peppers, and celery in the oil for 10 minutes using a soup pot.
3. Whisk the rest of the ingredients, including the roux, into the soup pot and bring the entire mixture to a boil.
4. After the mixture has boiled, reduce the heat and let it simmer for another 5 minutes.
5. Season the soup as you like with salt and pepper. To serve, ladle the soup evenly into the prepared bread bowls and sprinkle with fresh chives, if desired.

# Wolfgang Puck's Butternut Squash Soup

Creamy squash soup is always delicious. This butternut squash soup is the perfect appetizer you've been looking for.

*Makes: 2 quarts – Preparation Time: 25 min. – Cooking Time: 1 h 20 min.*
*Nutrition facts per batch: Calories 1293.8, Total Fat 64.3 g, Carbs 172.8 g,*
*Protein 27.9 g, Sodium 1296.3 mg*

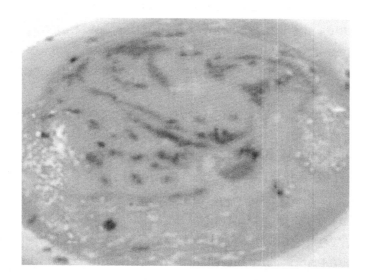

## *Ingredients*
Soup:
3¾ pounds butternut squash
1¾ pounds acorn squash
6 tablespoons unsalted butter, divided
1 onion, finely diced
½ teaspoon kosher salt
⅛ teaspoon fresh white pepper
¼ teaspoon ground nutmeg
¼ teaspoon ginger, ground
⅛ teaspoon ground cardamom
4 cups chicken or vegetable stock, warmed
½ cup crème fraiche

1 tablespoon thinly sliced fresh chives

Roasted Red Pepper Coulis
2 red bell peppers
¼ cup chicken broth
Salt and pepper

***Preparation***
1. Preheat the oven to 350°F. Melt 2 tablespoons of the butter and season with salt, pepper, and nutmeg.
2. Prepare the squashes by cutting them in half, removing the seeds, and brushing the cut sides with the seasoned butter.
3. Line the squashes, cut-side down, on a baking pan. Bake for an hour.
4. When the squashes are soft, scoop them out into a bowl and purée. Set the squash purée aside.
5. Sauté the onions in 4 tablespoons of butter over low heat. Do not let them turn brown.
6. When the onions become translucent, add in the squash purée and allow the mixture to continue cooking. Make sure that the mixture does not simmer or boil.
7. When the mixture is heated through, add in the ginger and cardamom, then pour in the stock.
8. Without increasing the heat, bring the mixture to a boil. Allow the mixture to cook for 20 minutes while stirring occasionally.
9. Meanwhile, make the red pepper coulis:
    a) Roast the bell peppers over flame until the skin is charred or in oven under the broiler. Let the pepper cool down.
    b) Peel of the skin of the peppers and then purée the flesh while slowly pouring in the chicken broth.
    c) Season with salt and pepper.
    d) Transfer to a sauce bottle and set aside.

10. When the mixture has cooked through, add in the crème fraiche and chives.
11. When the flavors have mixed, remove the rosemary sprig and season the soup to your liking.
12. Transfer the mixture to a bowl and squeeze the red pepper coulis over the soup, creating swirls before serving.

# Copycat Chicken Recipes

## Chipotle's Chicken

This entrée is sure to be a hit at your next party. Or family dinner. Or whatever you choose! It's simple yet tasty.

*Serves: 8 – Prep. Time: 10 min. – Marinate Time: 24 h – Cooking Time: 20 min. Nutrition facts per serving: Calories 293, Total Fat 18.7 g, Carbs 5.8 g, Protein 24.9 g, Sodium 526 mg*

**Ingredients**
2 ½ pound organic boneless and skinless chicken breasts or thighs
Olive oil or cooking spray

Marinade
7 oz. chipotle peppers in adobo sauce
2 tablespoons olive oil

6 garlic cloves, peeled
1 teaspoon black pepper
2 teaspoons salt
½ teaspoon cumin
½ teaspoon dry oregano

## *Preparation*

1. Pour all the marinade ingredients in a food processor or blender and blend until you get a smooth paste.
2. Pound the chicken until it has a thickness between ½ to ¾ inch. Place chicken into an airtight container or re-sealable plastic bag such as a Ziploc. Pour the marinade over the chicken and stir until well coated. Place the chicken in the refrigerator and let marinate overnight or up to 24 hours.
3. Pour the blended mixture into the container and marinate the chicken for at least 8 hours.
4. Cook the chicken over medium to high heat on an oiled and preheated grill for 3 to 5 minutes per side. The internal temperature of the chicken should be 165°F before you remove it from the heat. You can also cook it in heavy bottomed skillet over medium heat with a little olive oil.
5. Let rest before serving. If desired, cut into cubes to add to salads, tacos or quesadillas or serve as is.

# Popeye's Fried Chicken

Fried chicken is a classic dish for the kids. If your kids love Popeye's version, then here's a recipe that you can do right in your kitchen.

*Serves: 8 – Preparation Time: 20 minutes – Cooking Time: 45 minutes*
*Nutrition facts per serving: Calories 733, Total Fat 26.8 g, Carbs 76.3 g, Protein 44.3 g, Sodium 3140 mg*

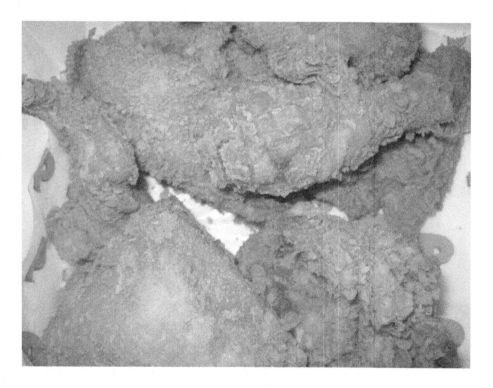

## Ingredients
Breading:
3 cups self-rising flour
1 cup corn starch
3 tablespoons seasoning salt
2 tablespoons paprika
1 teaspoon baking soda
1 package (0.7 ounce) dry Italian-style salad dressing mix

1 package (1 ounce) dry onion soup mix

1 (1 ½ ounces) packet dry spaghetti sauce spices and seasoning mix

3 tablespoons white sugar

Batter/Coating:

3 cups cornflakes cereal, crushed

2 eggs, beaten

¼ cup cold water

Chicken:

2 cups oil for frying

1 (4-pound) whole chicken, cut into pieces

### Preparation

1. Mix all of the breading ingredients together in a deep bowl.
2. Place the crushed cereal in another bowl.
3. In another bowl, beat the eggs and cold water together.
4. Heat the oil to 350°F and preheat the oven to 350°F.
5. Dip the chicken into the breading mixture, the egg mixture, the crushed cereal, and then the breading mixture again.
6. Immediately place the breaded chicken into the heated oil and cook on each side for 3 to 4 minutes.
7. Place the chicken in a 9×13 baking pan skin-side up. Cover the baking pan with foil, leaving a small opening.
8. Bake the chicken for 45 minutes.
9. After 45 minutes, remove the foil and continue baking for another 5 minutes.
10. Remove the baking pan from the oven and serve.

# McDonald's Chicken Nuggets

Chicken nuggets are tasty, but kind of unhealthy. This all-natural recipe will give you a healthy alternative to the McDonald's version.

*Serves: 4 – Preparation Time: 1 hour 45 minutes – Cooking Time: 45 minutes*
*Nutrition facts per serving: Calories 370.5, Total Fat 5 g, Carbs 44.9 g,*
*Protein 33.2 g, Sodium 1457.4 mg*

## Ingredients
Chicken:
1 pound chicken tenderloins, boneless and thawed

Brine:
4 cups water, cold
2 teaspoons fine sea salt

Breading:

⅓ + ½ cup all-purpose flour, sifted
All-purpose flour, sifted
½ cup corn starch
1½ tablespoons seasoned salt
1 tablespoon fine corn flour
1½ teaspoons dry milk powder, non-fat
1 teaspoon granulated sugar
½ teaspoon ginger, ground
¼ teaspoon mustard, ground
¼ teaspoon black pepper, fine
¼ teaspoon white pepper, fine
⅛ teaspoon allspice, ground
⅛ teaspoon cloves, ground
⅛ teaspoon paprika, ground
⅛ teaspoon turmeric, ground
1 pinch cinnamon, ground
1 pinch cayenne pepper

Batter:

2 eggs, beaten
½ cup water, cold
2 tablespoons corn starch
2 tablespoons all-purpose flour
¼ teaspoon sea salt, fine
¼ teaspoon sesame oil
¼ teaspoon soy sauce
¼ teaspoon granulated sugar

For Deep Frying:

Vegetable oil, 3 parts
Vegetable shortening, 1 part

### Preparation

1. Pound the chicken until it is only ½ inch thick.
2. Mix the brine ingredients.
3. Cut the chicken into small, chicken-nugget-sized pieces and place them in the brine. Leave it in the refrigerator for 2 hours.
4. When the chicken is almost done soaking, whisk together all the batter ingredients. Also mix together all the breading ingredients.
5. Remove the chicken from the refrigerator and evenly coat each piece with the batter.
6. Evenly coat each battered piece with the breading.
7. Slowly heat the deep-frying ingredients to 350°F.
8. Deep fry each nugget and then transfer to a plate with a paper towel to drain the oil.
9. Transfer to a different plate and serve.
10. Note: The nuggets can be battered up and breaded in advance and stored in an airtight container if you want to fry them later

# Ruby Tuesday's Sonora Chicken Pasta

Pasta is both filling and delicious. Here is a quick meal that you can make whenever you want some comfort food.

*Serves: 4 – Preparation Time: 25 minutes – Cooking Time: 20 minutes*
*Nutrition facts per serving: Calories 966, Total Fat 18 g, Carbs 34 g,*
*Protein 0 g, Sodium 0 mg*

### *Ingredients*
Cheese Mixture
1 pound processed cheese like Velveeta
½ cup heavy cream
2 teaspoons olive oil
2 tablespoons red chili peppers, minced
2 tablespoons green chili peppers, minced

2 tablespoons onions, minced
½ garlic clove, minced
2 tablespoons water
¼ teaspoon salt
2 teaspoons sugar
½ tablespoon vinegar
¼ teaspoon cumin

Beans
1 can 15-ounce can black beans, with the water
2 tablespoons green chili peppers, minced
2 tablespoons onions, minced
½ garlic clove, minced
¼ teaspoon salt

1 dash paprika

Seasoning and Chicken:
Vegetable oil
½ teaspoon salt
1 dash dried thyme
1 dash dried summer savory
4 chicken breast halves, boneless, skinless

Pasta:
1 box (16 ounces) penne pasta
4 quarts water
1 tablespoon butter

Garnish:
Green onion, chopped
Tomatoes, diced

## Preparation

1. Preheat your grill.
2. Mix the Velveeta and the cream over heat until smooth.
3. In another pan, heat the olive oil and sauté the peppers, onions, and garlic clove.
4. After 2 minutes, add the water and bring to a simmer for another 2 minutes.
5. Add the sautéed vegetables to the cheese and continue simmering over low heat. Add in the salt, the sugar, the vinegar, and the cumin, and leave the entire mixture over low heat. Make sure to stir.
6. In another saucepan, bring the beans, peppers, onions, garlic, salt, and paprika to a boil over medium heat.
7. When the bean mixture starts boiling, reduce the heat to low and keep it simmering.
8. Mix all the seasoning ingredients and then rub the seasoning all over the chicken.
9. Cook the chicken in oil thoroughly, for 5 minutes on each side, and then slice the chicken pieces into ½-inch slices.
10. Boil the pasta in the water. When it is cooked, drain the pasta and mix in the butter while the noodles are still hot.
11. Assemble the dish by covering the pasta in sauce, placing the bean mixture over it, and then adding the chicken. Garnish the dish by topping everything with the tomatoes and green onions.

# Olive Garden's Parmesan Crusted Chicken

This pasta has a crunchy twist that satisfies the taste buds. And you can make it in under an hour!

*Serves: 4 – Preparation Time: 15 minutes – Cooking Time: 40 minutes*
*Nutrition facts per serving: Calories 1231, Total Fat 60.4 g, Carbs 128.7 g,*
*Protein 33.4 g, Sodium 1406.1 mg*

## Ingredients
Breading:
1 cup plain breadcrumbs
2 tablespoons flour
¼ cup grated parmesan cheese

For dipping:
1 cup milk

Chicken:
2 chicken breasts
Vegetable oil for frying
2 cups cooked linguini pasta
2 tablespoons butter
3 tablespoons olive oil

2 teaspoons crushed garlic
½ cup white wine
¼ cup water
2 tablespoons flour
¾ cup half-and-half
¼ cup sour cream
½ teaspoon salt
1 teaspoon fresh flat leave parsley, finely diced¾ cup mild Asiago cheese, finely grated

Garnish:
1 Roma tomato, diced
Grated parmesan cheese
Fresh flat leaf parsley, finely chopped

**Preparation**
1. Pound the chicken until it flattens to ½ inch thick.
2. Mix the breading ingredients in one shallow bowl and place the milk in another.
3. Heat some oil over medium to medium-to-low heat.
4. Dip the chicken in the breading, then the milk, then the breading again. immediately place into heated oil.
5. Cook the chicken in the oil until golden brown, about 3-4 minutes per side. Remove the chicken and set aside on a plate lined with paper towels.
6. Create a roux by adding flour to heated olive oil and butter over medium heat.
7. When the roux is done, add the garlic, water, and salt to the pan and stir.
8. Add the wine and continue stirring and cooking.
9. Add the half-and-half and sour cream and stir some more.
10. Add the cheese and let it melt.
11. Finally, add in the parsley and remove from heat. Add pasta and stir to coat.
12. Divide the hot pasta between serving plates.
13. Top each dish with the chicken, diced tomatoes, and parmesan cheese before serving.

# Olive Garden's Chicken Marsala

A classic staple from one of America's favorite Italian restaurants that is easy to prepare and so delicious.

*Serves: 4-6 – Preparation Time: 10 minutes – Cooking Time: 40 minutes*
*Nutrition facts per serving: Calories 950, Total Fat 58 g, Carbs 71 g,*
*Protein 66 g, Sodium 1910 mg*

### Ingredients
2 tablespoons olive oil
2 tablespoons butter
4 boneless skinless chicken breasts
1 ½ cups sliced mushrooms
1 small clove garlic, thinly sliced
Flour for dredging
Sea salt and freshly ground black pepper
1 ½ cups chicken stock
1 ½ cups Marsala wine

1 tablespoon lemon juice
1 teaspoon Dijon mustard

## *Preparation*
Chicken scaloppini
1. Pound out the chicken with a mallet or rolling pin to about
   ½ inch thick
2. In a large skillet, heat the olive oil and 1 tablespoon of the
   butter over medium-high heat. When the oil is hot, dredge
   the chicken in flour. Season with salt and pepper on both
   sides. Dredge only as many as will fit in the skillet. Don't
   overcrowd the pan.
3. Cook chicken in batches, about 1 to 2 minutes on each
   side or until cooked through. Remove from skillet, and
   place on an oven-proof platter. Keep warm, in oven, while
   remaining chicken is cooked.

Marsala sauce
1. In the same skillet, add 1 tablespoon of olive oil. On
   medium-high heat, sauté mushrooms and garlic until
   softened. Remove the mushrooms from the pan and set
   aside.
2. Add the chicken stock and loosen any remaining bits in
   the pan. On high heat, let reduce by half, about 6-8
   minutes. Add Marsala wine and lemon juice and in the
   same manner reduce by half, about 6–8 minutes. Add the
   mushroom back in the saucepan, and stir in the Dijon
   mustard. Warm for 1 minute on medium-low heat.
   Remove from heat, stir in the remaining butter to make
   the sauce silkier.
3. To serve, pour sauce over chicken, and serve
   immediately.

# Cracker Barrel's Green Chili Jack Chicken

If you want some spice in your next meal, try this on for size. This yummy chicken entrée will delight your taste buds.

*Serves: 2 – Preparation Time: 5 minutes – Cooking Time: 20 minutes*
*Nutrition facts per serving: Calories 516, Total Fat 24.4 g, Carbs 8.5 g,*
*Protein 64.2 g, Sodium 697.9 mg*

## *Ingredients*
1 pound chicken strips
1 teaspoon chili powder
4 ounces green chilies
2 cups Monterey Jack cheese, shredded
¼ cup salsa

## *Preparation*

1. Sprinkle the chicken with the chili powder while heating some oil over medium heat.
2. Cook the chicken strips until they are half cooked, and then place the green chilies on top of the chicken. Lower the heat to low.
3. Cook for 1 to 2 minutes before adding the cheese on top. Keep cooking the chicken and cheese until the cheese melts.
4. Serve the chicken with the salsa.

# Carrabba's Pollo Rosa Maria

If you're in love with Carrabba's Italian Grill, then you need to try their Pollo Rosa Maria. Make some of this healthy dish at home and share the recipe with your friends.

*Serves: 4 – Preparation Time: 5 minutes – Cooking Time: 50 minutes*
*Nutrition facts per serving: Calories 644.4, Total Fat 52.3 g, Carbs 6 g,*
*Protein 36 g, Sodium 248.2 mg*

## Ingredients
4 butterflied chicken breasts
4 slices prosciutto
4 slices Fontina cheese
½ cup clarified butter
3 garlic cloves
½ sweet onion, diced
¼ cup dry white wine
4 tablespoons unsalted butter

½ white pepper
1 dash salt
8 ounces cremini mushrooms, sliced
½ cup fresh basil, chopped
1 lemon, juiced
Shredded Parmesan for garnish

### *Preparation*

1. Grill the chicken breasts on each side for 3 to 5 minutes.
2. Remove the chicken from heat and then stuff with the prosciutto and cheese. Place the ham and cheese on one side of the chicken and fold it over. Secure the filling with a toothpick.
3. Wrap the chicken in foil to keep it warm.
4. Sauté the onions and garlic in butter until they become tender. Add the white wine to deglaze the pan.
5. In the same pan, sauté the mushrooms in the salt, pepper, and butter until tender, then add the remaining ingredients and cook until completely blended.
6. Transfer the chicken to a plate and pour the mushroom sauce over it. Remove the toothpick and serve. Garnish with Parmesan cheese, if desired

# Chili's Crispy Honey-Chipotle Chicken Crispers

Sometimes, fried chicken is the only way to go. Make this simple recipe at home and your family and stomach will thank you.

*Serves: 4 – Preparation Time: 15 minutes – Cooking Time: 30 minutes*
*Nutrition facts per serving: Calories 492, Total Fat 3.3 g, Carbs 107.2 g,*
*Protein 11.2 g, Sodium 2331.5 mg*

### *Ingredients*
Chicken: 12 chicken tenderloins
Some shortening or 6 cups vegetable oil for frying

Honey-Chipotle Sauce:
⅔ cup honey
¼ cup water

¼ cup ketchup
1 tablespoon white vinegar
2 teaspoons chipotle chili pepper, ground or powdered
½ teaspoon salt

Batter:
1 egg, beaten
½ cup whole milk
½ cup chicken broth
1½ teaspoons salt
¼ teaspoon black pepper
¼ teaspoon paprika
¼ teaspoon garlic powder
¾ cup all-purpose flour

Breading:
1½ cups all-purpose flour
1½ teaspoons salt
¾ teaspoon paprika
½ teaspoon black pepper
½ teaspoon garlic powder

Garnish
French fries
Corn on the cub
Ranch dipping sauce

**Preparation**

1. Mix together all the chipotle sauce ingredients in a saucepan and bring to a boil over medium heat. When the sauce starts boiling, reduce it to a simmer and leave it for another two minutes before removing from heat.
2. Preheat the oil to 350°F. While you are waiting for your oil to heat, whisk all the batter ingredients (except the flour) together for 30 seconds, or until thoroughly mixed. When everything is mixed, add in the flour and mix again.
3. Add all the breading ingredients to another bowl.

4. Place the batter and breading bowls beside each other to make your coating station. The oil should be hot enough now.
5. Dip the chicken into the batter, let the excess batter drip off, and then dip it in the breading to coat.
6. Place the breaded chicken on a plate and start frying, two at a time at most. Leave each chicken piece in the oil for at least 4 minutes.
7. Prepare a plate by covering it with paper towels.
8. When the chicken is done cooking, transfer it to the paper towels to let the oil drain off.
9. Let the fried chicken cool, and then transfer it to a deep bowl. Add in the sauce and toss everything together. Make sure you cover the chicken in sauce.
10. Transfer to a plate and serve with sides of French fries, corn on the cub, and ranch dipping sauce.

# P.F. Chang's Crispy Honey Chicken

Nothing hits the spot quite like Asian honey chicken dishes. Make some of this dish right at home and enjoy the Asian comfort food.

*Serves: 4 – Preparation Time: 20 minutes – Cooking Time: 2 hours*
*Nutrition facts per serving: Calories 680.3, Total Fat 12 g, Carbs 104.8 g,*
*Protein 30.7 g, Sodium 1299.6 mg*

### Ingredients
Chicken:
1 pound chicken breast, boneless, skinless, cut into medium sized chunks
Vegetable oil, for frying and deep frying

Batter:
4 ounces all-purpose flour
2½ ounces cornstarch
1 egg
6 ounces water

⅛ teaspoon baking powder
⅛ teaspoon baking soda

Chicken Seasoning:
1 tablespoon light soy sauce
⅛ teaspoon white pepper
¼ teaspoon kosher salt
1 tablespoon cornstarch

Sauce:
½ cup sake or rice wine
½ cup honey
3 ounces rice vinegar
3 tablespoons light soy sauce
6 tablespoons sugar
¼ cup cornstarch
¼ cup water

**Preparation**
1. Make the batter at least 2 hours in advance.
2. Mix all the batter ingredients together and refrigerate.
3. After an hour and 40 minutes, mix all the seasoning ingredients together and mix in the chicken. Make sure that the chicken is covered entirely.
4. Place the chicken in the refrigerator to marinate for at least 20 minutes.
5. Mix all the sauce ingredients together (except the cornstarch and water) and set aside.
6. Before you begin frying your chicken:
   a) Place a paper towel on a plate in preparation for draining the oil; and
   b) Heat your oil to 350°F.
7. When your oil is heated, remove the chicken from the refrigerator and pour the batter all over it.

8. One by one, lower the coated chicken pieces into the heated oil. Keep them suspended until the batter is cooked (20 to 30 seconds).
9. When all the chicken is cooked, place it on the plate covered with the paper towel to cool and drain.
10. Bring the sauce mixture to a boil. While waiting for it to boil, mix the cornstarch and water in a separate bowl.
11. Slowly pour the cornstarch mixture into the sauce and continue cooking for 2 minutes, until the sauce thickens.
12. When the sauce thickens, remove it from heat.
13. When the chicken is cooked, pour some sauce over the entire mixture, just enough to cover the chicken.
14. Transfer everything to a plate with rice or Chinese noodles and serve.

# Boston Market's Chicken Pot Pie

This small dish is both filing and satisfying. In under an hour, you can make an entire meal!

*Serves: 4 – Preparation Time: 10 minutes – Cooking Time: 40 minutes*
*Nutrition facts per serving: Calories 450, Total Fat 30 g, Carbs 35 g,*
*Protein 10 g, Sodium 680 mg*

## *Ingredients*
1 cup half-and-half
1 cup chicken broth
3 tablespoons all-purpose flour
2 cups shredded chicken breast, roasted, skinless
2 cups mixed frozen vegetables, thawed
2 tablespoons fresh flat-leaf parsley, chopped
2 tablespoons chives, chopped
1 teaspoon fresh thyme, chopped
1 teaspoon lemon juice

1 teaspoon salt
½ teaspoon lemon zest, grated
½ teaspoon freshly ground black pepper
7 ounces ready-to-use refrigerated pie crust

## Preparation

1. Get ready by:
   a) Preheating the oven to 425°F;
   b) Lightly flouring a flat surface; and
   c) Bringing out 4 10-ounce ramekins.
2. Bring the half-and-half, broth, and flour to a boil while stirring with a whisk.
3. Reduce the heat and continue to simmer for another 4 minutes while continuing to whisk the mixture.
4. When the mixture thickens, add the remaining ingredients into the mix, except the pie crust.
5. When all the ingredients are cooked, turn off the heat and cover the pan. Set the mixture aside to work on the pie crust.
6. Place the pie crust on your floured surface and roll it into a circle with an 11-inch diameter. Cut the crust into quarters.
7. Scoop the warm chicken mixture into each of the ramekins. Cover the tops with the pie crust, letting it drape over the edges. Slice an X into each of the tops to allow the pie to cook completely.
8. Bake the pies for 25 minutes and remove from the oven. Let rest 10 minutes before serving.

# Copycat Beef and Pork Recipes

## P.F. Chang's Beef and Broccoli

This healthy and tasty dish will satisfy more of your Asian cravings. With this recipe, you can make your favorite classic Asian dish in the comfort of your own home.

*Serves: 4 – Preparation Time: 45 minutes – Cooking Time: 15 minutes*
*Nutrition facts per serving: Calories 331, Total Fat 21.1 g, Carbs 13.3 g,*
*Protein 21.7 g, Sodium 419 mg*

## Ingredients

Marinade:

⅓ cup oyster sauce

2 teaspoons toasted sesame oil

⅓ cup sherry

1 teaspoon soy sauce

1 teaspoon white sugar

1 teaspoon corn starch


Beef and Broccoli:

¾ pound beef round steak, cut into ⅛-inch thick strips

3 tablespoons vegetable oil

1 thin slice of fresh ginger root

1 clove garlic, peeled and smashed

1 pound broccoli, cut into florets

## Preparation

1. Mix the marinade ingredients in a bowl until they have dissolved.
2. Marinate the beef in the mixture for 30 minutes.
3. Sauté the ginger and garlic in hot oil for a minute.
4. When the oil is flavored, remove the garlic and ginger and add in the broccoli. Continue cooking the broccoli until tender.
5. When the broccoli is cooked, transfer it to a bowl and set aside. Pour the beef and the marinade into the pan in which you cooked the broccoli and continue cooking until beef is cooked, or about 5 minutes.
6. Pour the broccoli back in and keep cooking for another 3 minutes.
7. Transfer to a bowl or plate and serve.

# Taco Bell's Chalupa

Chalupas are both simple *and* fun to make. Prepare the ingredients and assemble this dish with friends for a meaningful meal at home.

*Serves: 8 – Preparation Time: 40 minutes – Cooking Time: 10 minutes
Nutrition facts per serving: Calories 424.9, Total Fat 15.8 g, Carbs 47.7 g,
Protein 21.6 g, Sodium 856.8 mg*

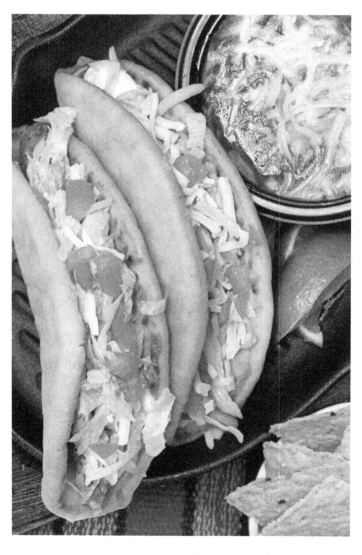

### Ingredients

Tortillas:

2½ cups flour
1 tablespoon baking powder
½ teaspoon salt
1 tablespoon vegetable shortening
1 cup milk
Oil, for deep frying

Filling:

1 tablespoon dried onion flakes
½ cup water
1 pound ground beef
¼ cup flour
1 tablespoon chili powder
1 teaspoon paprika
1 teaspoon salt
Some oil for frying

For Garnishing:

Some sour cream
Some lettuce, shredded
Some cheddar cheese or Monterey Jack cheese
Some tomato, diced

### Preparation

1. In a bowl, mix the flour, baking powder, and salt together.
2. Add the vegetable shortening and mix. Then add the milk and continue mixing.
3. Cut the dough into 8 equal portions, and then shape them into 8 6-inch tortillas.
4. Deep fry the tortillas until golden brown. Set aside to cool.
5. Start making the filling. Place the onion flakes in the water and set aside for 5 minutes.

6. Mix the rest of the filling ingredients (except the oil) together until combined.
7. Add in the onion with the water and continue mixing.
8. Heat the oil in a skillet, and then cook the entire beef mixture until the beef browns.
9. Now, assemble your Chalupas. In the tortillas, place the following by layers:
   a) Cooked beef mixture;
   b) Sour cream;
   c) Lettuce;
   d) Cheese; and lastly
   e) Tomatoes.
10. Serve on a plate.

# Outback's Secret Seasoning Mix for Steaks

Steak is always a crowd pleaser. Make it just right and satisfy hungry guests.

*Yields 3 ½ tablespoons– Preparation Time: 5 min. – Cooking Time: 10 min.*
*Nutrition facts (spice blend only): Calories 16.4, Total Fat 0.5 g, Carbs 3.5 g, Protein 0.7 g, Sodium 2328.4 mg*

## Ingredients
Seasoning:
4–6 teaspoons salt
4 teaspoons paprika
2 teaspoons ground black pepper
1 teaspoon onion powder
1 teaspoon garlic powder
1 teaspoon cayenne pepper
½ teaspoon coriander
½ teaspoon turmeric

## Preparation
1. Mix all the seasoning ingredients in a small bowl. Rub the spice blend into the meat on all sides and let rest for 15-20 minutes before cooking.

# Chili's Baby Back Ribs

If you get them just right, ribs are amazing. Make these ribs and serve them at your next house party for a room full of happy guests.

*Serves: 4 – Preparation Time: 15 min. – Cooking Time: 3 hours 30 min.*
*Nutrition facts per serving: Calories 645, Total Fat 43.8 g, Carbs 10.8 g,*
*Protein 51.5 g, Sodium 530 mg*

**Ingredients**
Pork:
4 racks baby-back pork ribs

Sauce:
1½ cups water
1 cup white vinegar
½ cup tomato paste
1 tablespoon yellow mustard
⅔ cup dark brown sugar packed

1 teaspoon hickory flavored liquid smoke
1½ teaspoons salt
½ teaspoon onion powder
¼ teaspoon garlic powder
¼ teaspoon paprika

## *Preparation*

1. Mix together all of the sauce ingredients and then bring to a boil.
2. When the sauce starts to boil, reduce it to a simmer. Continue simmering the mixture for 45 to 60 minutes, mixing occasionally. When the sauce is almost done, preheat the oven to 300°F.
3. Choose a flat surface and lay some aluminum foil over it, enough to cover 1 rack of ribs. Place the ribs on top.
4. Remove the sauce from heat and start brushing it all over the ribs.
5. When the rack is completely covered, wrap it with the aluminum foil and place it on the baking pan with the opening of the foil facing upwards.
6. Repeat steps 3 to 5 for the remaining racks.
7. Bake the ribs for 2½ hours.
8. When they are almost done baking, preheat your grill to medium heat.
9. Grill both sides of each rack for 4 to 8 minutes. When you are almost done grilling, brush some more sauce over each side and grill for a few more minutes. Make sure that the sauce doesn't burn.
10. Transfer the racks to a large plate and serve with extra sauce.

# Applebee's Honey Barbecue Sauce with Riblets

Another ribs recipe to satisfy your cravings. When they fall off the bone, you know that they are perfect.

*Serves: 4 – Preparation Time: 20 min. – Cooking Time: 3 hours 30 min. Nutrition facts per serving: Calories 1110, Total Fat 57 g, Carbs 89.3 g, Protein 63 g, Sodium 3360 mg*

**Ingredients**
Honey Barbecue Sauce:
1 cup ketchup
½ cup corn syrup
½ cup honey
¼ cup apple cider vinegar

¼ cup water
2 tablespoons molasses
2 teaspoons dry mustard
2 teaspoons garlic powder
1 teaspoon chili powder
1 teaspoon onion powder

Meat:
2¼ pounds pork riblets
Salt
Pepper
Garlic
¼ teaspoon liquid smoke flavoring
1 teaspoon water

**Preparation**
1. Season the riblets with the salt, garlic, and pepper based on your preferences, then sear them on a grill until the meat starts to separate from the bone. While doing this, preheat the oven to 275°F.
2. Mix the water and liquid smoke flavoring into a deep pan and place the ribs on an elevated rack inside—make sure that the liquid *does not* touch the ribs.
3. Cover the pan with two layers of foil and bake for 2 to 5 hours, depending on the strength of your oven and the number of riblets you have. Make sure that the internal temperature of the meat reaches 155°F all throughout.
4. While waiting for the riblets to cook, prepare the sauce by mixing all of the sauce ingredients together and simmering for 20 minutes.
5. When the sauce is done cooking, transfer to a bowl and set aside.
6. When the ribs are done cooking, sear them on a grill until the marrow starts sizzling.
7. Place the ribs on a plate and cover generously with the sauce.
8. Serve and enjoy.

# Cracker Barrel's Green Beans with Bacon

This healthy meal gets a kick of flavor from bacon. Prepare this simple yet delicious dish to add some vegetables to your table.

*Serves: 6 – Preparation Time: 10 minutes – Cooking Time: 45 minutes*
*Nutrition facts per serving: Calories 155.3, Total Fat 9 g, Carbs 15.7 g,*
*Protein 6 g, Sodium 363.8 mg*

### *Ingredients*
¼ pound sliced bacon, cut into 1-inch pieces
3 cans (14.5 ounces each) green beans, with liquid
¼ yellow onion, peeled, chopped
1 teaspoon granulated sugar

½ teaspoon salt

½ teaspoon fresh ground black pepper

## *Preparation*

1. Half-cook the bacon in a saucepan—make sure it does not get crispy.
2. Add the green beans with the liquid to the browned bacon and season with salt, pepper, and sugar.
3. Top the green beans with the onion and then cover the pan until the mixture boils.
4. Lower the heat and allow the mixture to simmer for another 45 minutes before serving.

# Café Rio's Pork

This dish goes perfect with rice. Its tenderness and flavor will make your taste buds sing.

*Serves: 10 – Preparation Time: 10 minutes – Cooking Time: 9 hours*
*Nutrition facts per serving: Calories 317, Total Fat 7 g, Carbs 31 g,*
*Protein 28 g, Sodium 439 mg*

**Ingredients**
<u>For the Marinade:</u>
3 pounds boneless pork loin
12 ounces Coca Cola
¼ cup brown sugar

<u>For the Seasoning:</u>
1 teaspoon garlic salt
1 teaspoon onion salt
1 teaspoon chili powder
1 teaspoon cumin, ground
12 ounces Coca Cola

<u>For the Sauce:</u>
12 ounces Coca Cola
¾ cup brown sugar
½ teaspoon chili powder
½ teaspoon ground cumin
1 can (4 ounces) green chili, ground
1 can (10 ounces) red enchilada sauce

## *Preparation*

1. Mix the Coca Cola and sugar in an airtight container or sealable plastic bag to make the marinade.
2. Massage the marinade into the pork. Place it in the container to marinate for at least 8 hours.
3. Place the pork into a slow cooker and cover with all of the seasoning ingredients in the order specified. Cook the pork on low for 7 to 9 hours.
4. After cooking, shred the pork and remove the liquid from the slow cooker.
5. Return the shredded pork to the slow cooker.
6. Place all of the sauce ingredients in a food processor or blender. Blend well to create the sauce.
7. Pour the sauce over the pork, and then cook the entire mixture for another 30 minutes.
8. Transfer to a bowl and serve.

# Ruth Chris's Filet Mignon with Béarnaise Sauce

Cooked just right, filet mignon is one of the most delicious steaks known to man. With this simple recipe, you can make a delicious filet mignon for dinner.

*Serves: 4 – Preparation Time: 10 minutes – Cooking Time: 40 minutes*
*Nutrition facts per serving: Calories 340, Total Fat 8 g, Carbs 18 g,*
*Protein 201 g, Sodium 580 mg*

### Ingredients
Vinegar Reduction:
2 tablespoons tarragon vinegar
2 teaspoons fresh lemon juice
2 teaspoons shallots, finely chopped
1 teaspoon dried tarragon
Fresh ground black pepper, to taste

Sauce:
2 large egg yolks
¼ cup water
Salt, to taste
2 teaspoons fresh tarragon, chopped
2 teaspoons fresh chervil, chopped (optional)
½ cup unsalted butter, melted

Steak:
4 filet mignon steaks. about 8 ounces each

**Preparation**
1. Mix all of the vinegar reduction ingredients together and bring to a boil over medium to high heat.
2. When the vinegar mixture starts to boil, lower the heat and allow the mixture to simmer until most of the liquid evaporates.
3. When only small bubbles of liquid are left, remove the vinegar reduction from heat and set aside.
4. Bring some water to a simmer in the bottom part of a double boiler while whisking the egg yolks and water in the top part.
5. Place the top part over the simmering water, making sure that the water does not touch the bottom of the bowl.
6. Pour the vinegar reduction into the egg mixture and whisk until the entire mixture reaches 284°F.
7. Remove the mixture from heat, but continue whisking. Slowly pour in the melted butter while continuing to whisk the mixture.
8. Add in the remaining sauce ingredients and continue stirring.
9. Set the Béarnaise sauce aside, keeping it warm at 220°F.
10. Season the steaks with salt and pepper while preheating the broiler for 10 minutes.
11. Broil the steaks to your preference (rare, medium rare, medium well, well done).
12. Transfer the steaks to a warm plate, add ¼ cup of Béarnaise sauce, and serve.

# P.F. Chang's Spare Ribs

Asian spare ribs are special—the flavor is undoubtedly one of a kind. Prepare this dish for your next meal if you are in an Oriental mood.

*Serves: 2 – Preparation Time: 5 minutes – Cooking Time: 25 minutes*
*Nutrition facts per serving: Calories 1344, Total Fat 77.2 g, Carbs 113.2 g,*
*Protein 52.5 g, Sodium 1557 mg*

***Ingredients***
Sauce:
1 cup ketchup
1 cup light corn syrup
½ cup hoisin sauce
½ cup water
⅓ cup light brown sugar, packed
2 tablespoons onions, minced
1 tablespoon rice vinegar

Ribs:

12 to 16 cups water

2 teaspoons salt

1 rack pork spareribs

4 cups vegetable oil

1 teaspoon sesame seeds, for garnish

1 tablespoon green onion, diced, for garnish

## *Preparation*

1. Mix all of the sauce ingredients together and bring to a boil. When the sauce starts to boil, reduce it to a simmer for 5 minutes. Set aside.
2. Place the water and salt into a large pot or Dutch oven and bring to a boil. While the water is coming to a boil, clean the spare ribs, removing the excess fat.
3. When the water is boiling, place all the ribs into the water and continue boiling for 12 to 14 minutes.
4. Drain and set aside.
5. While the ribs are cooling, heat the oil to 375°F. Prepare a plate by covering it with a paper towel.
6. When the oil is hot enough, place 4 to 6 ribs in it and fry for 6 minutes.
7. Repeat step 6 until all the ribs are fried.
8. Mix the fried ribs and the sauce over medium heat. Simmer for at least a minute.
9. Transfer the ribs to a plate or bowl and serve with rice. Garnish the ribs with the sesame seeds and green onions.

# Boston Market's Meatloaf

Usually, when you hear meatloaf, you think *bad*. Well, prepare to have a schema change. This meatloaf will disprove all your past misconceptions.

*Serves: 8 – Preparation Time: 10 minutes – Cooking Time: 1 hour 25 minutes*
*Nutrition facts per serving: Calories 210.1, Total Fat 10.9 g, Carbs 8.8 g,*
*Protein 18.3 g, Sodium 446.9 mg*

## Ingredients

Sauce:

1 cup tomato sauce

1½ tablespoons barbecue sauce

1 tablespoon sugar

Meatloaf:

1½ pounds lean ground sirloin

6 tablespoons all-purpose flour

¾ teaspoon salt

½ teaspoon onion powder

¼ teaspoon ground black pepper

1 dash garlic powder

## Preparation

1. To get started:
   a) Preheat the oven to 400°F; and
   b) Place the ground sirloin into a bowl.
2. Mix the sauce ingredients together and bring to a simmer over medium heat. When the sauce is simmering, remove it from heat.
3. Set aside 2 tablespoons of the sauce and pour the rest over the meat. Massage the sauce into the meat, marinating it well.
4. Add the rest of the meatloaf ingredients into the meat mixture and continue mixing and kneading until the spices are fully incorporated into the meat.
5. Place the meat into your loaf pan and cover with foil. Bake the meat mixture for 30 minutes.
6. Remove the pan from the oven and drain the fat before cutting the meatloaf into 8 equal portions.
7. Pour the set-aside sauce over the top of the meatloaf and return it to the oven for another 25 to 30 minutes.
8. Transfer the meatloaf to a plate and let cool before serving.

# Chili's Original Chili

There's nothing like a delicious bowl of hot chili. Make this dish for your next meal

*Serves: 4 – Preparation Time: 30 minutes – Cooking Time: 4 to 8 hours*
*Nutrition facts per serving: Calories 400, Total Fat 28 g, Carbs 14 g,*
*Protein 23 g, Sodium 1050 mg*

**Ingredients**
Spice Blend:
½ cup chili powder
⅛ cup salt
⅛ cup ground cumin
1 tablespoon paprika
1 teaspoon ground black pepper
1 teaspoon garlic powder
1 teaspoon of cayenne pepper

Chili:

4 pounds chuck, ground for chili

3¼ cups water

16 ounces tomato sauce

1½ cups yellow onions, chopped

1 tablespoon cooking oil

Masa Harina:

1 cup water

1 tablespoon masa harina

Sliced green onions for garnish, if desired

## Preparation

1. Place all of the spice blend ingredients in a bowl. Mix thoroughly and set the bowl aside.
2. Cook the meat over medium heat in a stock pot until it is brown. While the meat is cooking, thoroughly mix together the spice mix, water, and tomato sauce.
3. Add the spice mixture to the browned meat and bring to a boil.
4. While the chili is coming to a boil, sauté the onions in oil over medium heat.
5. When the chili is boiling and the onions are translucent, add the onions to the chili and stir.
6. Reduce the heat to low and allow the chili to simmer for an hour, stirring the mixture every 15 minutes.
7. In a bowl, mix the masa harina ingredients together. When the chili has been cooking for an hour, add the masa harina mixture to the chili and cook for another 10 minutes.
8. Transfer the chili to a bowl, garnish green onions, if desired, and serve.

# Black Angus Steakhouse's BBQ Baby Back Ribs

Here's another rib recipe if the other two weren't enough for you. Remember, falling-off-the-bone with perfection.

*Serves: 1 slab – Preparation Time: 30 minutes – Cooking Time: 6 to 8 hours*
*Nutrition facts per serving: Calories 1500, Total Fat 30 g, Carbs 108 g,*
*Protein 14 g, Sodium 3540 mg*

### *Ingredients*
1 rack of pork ribs
Your favorite barbecue sauce
Onion powder, to taste
Garlic powder, to taste

Marinade:
2 tablespoons kosher salt
2 tablespoons paprika

4 tablespoons granulated garlic

1 tablespoon onion powder

1 teaspoon cumin seeds

1 teaspoon Durkee Ancho pepper

2 teaspoons dry mustard

2 teaspoons black pepper

Rib Mop:

1 cup red wine vinegar

1 tablespoon garlic

1 cup water

3 tablespoons soy sauce

**Preparation**

1. Mix all of the marinade ingredients together.
2. Rub the marinade all over the ribs to soak them in flavor.
3. Barbecue the meat over indirect heat at 250°F to 300°F for 3 to 4 hours. Add soaked fruit wood to the coals for additional aroma. Make sure that the temperature remains at 250°F to 300°F for the entire cooking duration.
4. While the meat is cooking, mix together the rib mop ingredients in a bowl.
5. After three to four hours, transfer the meat to an aluminum pan and brush both sides with the rib mop.
6. Cook the ribs for another hour and then remove them from heat and mop them again. Continue cooking the ribs for another 3 to 4 hours, basting them with the mop and some barbecue sauce every hour.
7. When the ribs are done barbecuing, sprinkle them with onion and garlic powder before wrapping them in aluminum foil. Let the ribs rest for 30 minutes.
8. Transfer the ribs to a plate and serve.

# Texas Road House's Mesquite Grilled Pork Chops with Cinnamon Apples

Usually, you don't eat fruit with meat. But in this dish, the pairing is like fireworks in your mouth.

*Serves: 2 – Preparation Time: 40 minutes – Cooking Time: 40 minutes*
*Nutrition facts per serving: Calories 316, Total Fat 22.5 g, Carbs 9.1 g,*
*Protein 20.5 g, Sodium 2007.8 mg*

## *Ingredients*
Cinnamon Apples:
4 apples (peeled, sliced)
2 tablespoons butter, melted
⅓ cup brown sugar
2 tablespoons lemon juice
¾ teaspoon cinnamon

Pork Chop:
2 pork loin chops with bone, room temperature; 2 inches thick

<u>Paste:</u>
2 tablespoons extra virgin olive oil
2 tablespoons Worcestershire sauce
2 teaspoons black pepper, cracked
2 teaspoons chili powder
2 teaspoons granulated garlic powder
2 teaspoons kosher salt
1 teaspoon cumin, ground
½ teaspoon cinnamon, ground
Mesquite wood chips, soaked in water for at least 30 minutes

## *Preparation*

1. Prepare the apples by cooking all the cinnamon apple ingredients in butter until the apples soften.
2. When they are ready, set the cooked apples aside. Reheat before serving.
3. Before you begin with the meat, you need to:
   a) Soak the mesquite chips as instructed;
   b) Leave the pork loin at room temperature for 30 to 45 minutes; and
   c) Preheat the grill on high.
4. Thoroughly mix all the paste ingredients together. When the paste is done, spread it over the pork chops, covering them completely.
5. Remove the chips from the water and place them in an aluminum foil pan.
6. Place the pan directly over the fire from the grill and cook the pork loin on both sides for about 6 minutes. When the meat is seared, lower the heat to medium.
7. Place the pork over indirect medium heat and cook for another 25 minutes.
8. Remove the pork from heat, wrap it in aluminum foil, and let rest for another 5 minutes.
9. Transfer the pork to a plate with the reheated apples. Serve the entire dish.

# Copycat Fish and Seafood Recipes

## Applebee's Honey Grilled Salmon

This healthy salmon dish is something that you definitely need to try. Making it at home and customizing it to your tastes will make the dish even more perfect.

*Serves: 4 – Preparation Time: 10 minutes – Cooking Time: 30 minutes*
*Nutrition facts per serving: Calories 579.6, Total Fat 12.3 g, Carbs 70.5 g,*
*Protein 49 g, Sodium 1515.1 mg*

### Ingredients
Honey Pepper Sauce:
¾ cup honey
⅓ cup soy sauce
¼ cup dark brown sugar, packed

¼ cup pineapple juice

2 tablespoons fresh lemon juice

2 tablespoons white distilled vinegar

2 teaspoons olive oil

1 teaspoon black pepper, ground

½ teaspoon cayenne pepper

½ teaspoon paprika

¼ teaspoon garlic powder

Fish:

4 salmon fillets, 8 ounces each, skinned

## Preparation

1. Cook all of the sauce ingredients over medium to low heat until boiling. Once the mixture boils, lower the heat a little and allow it to simmer for another 15 minutes.
2. Rub the salmon with vegetable oil, salt, and pepper, and grill for 4 to 7 minutes on each side.
3. Serve with the honey pepper sauce.

# Red Lobster's Maple-Glazed Salmon and Shrimp

Here is another salmon recipe—except Red Lobster marries the delicious fish with some shrimp. If you like Red Lobster, here is one of their most amazing dishes.

*Serves: 4 – Preparation Time: 10 minutes – Cooking Time: 20 minutes*
*Nutrition facts per serving: Calories 364.7, Total Fat 7.4 g, Carbs 38.7 g,*
*Protein 34.8 g, Sodium 301.1 mg*

## Ingredients

⅔ cup maple syrup

½ cup water

2 tablespoons dried cherries, minced

1 tablespoon sugar

2 teaspoons soy sauce

1½ teaspoons lemon juice

24 pieces fresh medium shrimp, peeled

24 ounces salmon fillets

## Preparation

1. To get started:
   a) Skewer the shrimp on 4 skewers (i.e. 6 shrimp each);
   b) Season the shrimp with salt and pepper; and
   c) Season the salmon with salt and pepper.
2. Combine the maple syrup, water, cherries, sugar soy sauce and lemon juice and bring to a boil over medium heat. Reduce the heat and allow the mixture to simmer for another 8 to 10 minutes.
3. Grill the shrimp over high heat for 1 to 2 minutes per side. When you're done with the shrimp, grill the salmon over high heat for 3 to 4 minutes per side.
4. Arrange the shrimp and salmon on a plate and serve with the maple sauce.

# Chili's Garlic and Lime Shrimp

Shrimp and garlic is a perfect combination. Adding lime to the dish gives it that extra zest and freshness. Enjoy Chili's famous dish right in your own home.

*Serves: 4 – Preparation Time: 5 minutes – Cooking Time: 20 minutes*
*Nutrition facts per serving: Calories 89.1, Total Fat 6.3 g, Carbs 2.9 g,*
*Protein 6 g, Sodium 725.4 mg*

## *Ingredients*
Shrimp:
2 tablespoons butter
1 clove garlic, chopped
32 fresh medium shrimp, peeled
1 lime, halved

<u>Seasoning:</u>

¾ teaspoon salt

¼ teaspoon ground black pepper

¼ teaspoon cayenne pepper

¼ teaspoon dried parsley flakes

¼ teaspoon garlic powder

¼ teaspoon paprika

⅛ teaspoon dried thyme

⅛ teaspoon onion powder

## *Preparation*

1. Stir all the seasoning ingredients together to make the seasoning mix.
2. Sauté the garlic in the butter over medium heat for a few seconds before adding the shrimp to the pan. Squeeze the lime over the shrimp and continue to sauté it.
3. Stir in the seasoning mix, and continue sautéing the mixture for another 5 to 8 minutes.
4. Transfer to a plate and serve with thin lime wedges.

# Red Lobster's Nantucket Baked Cod

Baked cod in a special spice blend is always yummy. Here's Red Lobster's version of it. We hope you enjoy it.

*Serves: 4 – Preparation Time: 10 minutes – Cooking Time: 30 minutes*
*Nutrition facts per serving: Calories 187.9, Total Fat 4.9 g, Carbs 2.8 g,*
*Protein 31.9 g, Sodium 303.6 mg*

**Ingredients**
Fish:
4 fresh cod fish fillets, about 1 ½ pounds in total
1 tablespoon butter, melted
½ lemon, juiced
2 small tomatoes, sliced
2 tablespoons grated parmesan cheese

<u>Spice Blend:</u>
¼ teaspoon salt
¼ teaspoon paprika
1 dash black pepper
1 dash cayenne pepper

## *Preparation*
1. To get started:
   a) Preheat the oven to 450°F; and
   b) Prepare a 9×13 baking pan.
2. Place all the ingredients for the spice blend in a bowl and mix thoroughly.
3. Place the cod filets in the baking pan and brush with the tops with the butter.
4. Sprinkle the lemon juice and spice blend over the filets until you have finished all the spice blend.
5. Place 2 to 3 tomato slices on top of the spices for each fish.
6. Cover each slice of tomato with parmesan cheese.
7. Bake the fish for 8 minutes, then broil it on high for another 6 to 8 minutes.
8. Transfer the fish to a serving dish and serve with rice.

# Chili's Crunchy Fried Shrimp

Chili's has perfected the art of marrying protein with a perfect blend of spices, and we are sharing their expertise with you. Make some at home, adjusting the recipe to your liking.

*Serves: 8 – Preparation Time: 10 minutes – Cooking Time: 1 hour*
*Nutrition facts per serving: Calories 272.9, Total Fat 8.1 g, Carbs 28.7 g,*
*Protein 19.3 g, Sodium 854.2 mg*

### *Ingredients*
2 pounds large shrimp, peeled
Crisco shortening, melted
Corn flake crumbs

Batter:
⅔ cup flour
1⅓ cups cornstarch
½ teaspoon salt
½ teaspoon baking powder
6 egg whites

⅔ cup water

4 tablespoons vegetable oil

## *Preparation*

1. Mix the batter ingredients together and set aside.
2. In a separate container, pour out the cornflake crumbs.
3. Preheat the oil over medium heat.
4. Coat each shrimp with a generous amount of batter and then roll it in the crumbs.
5. Deep fry the shrimp until golden brown.
6. Place the shrimp on oil absorbent paper or paper towels.
7. Serve with cocktail or tartar sauce.

# Applebee's Garlic and Peppercorn Fried Shrimp

Almost all restaurants have their own version of fried and breaded shrimp, but Applebee's fried shrimp is in its own category. Try it out and discover a whole new level of deliciousness.

*Serves: 4 – Preparation Time: 5 minutes – Cooking Time: 30 minutes*
*Nutrition facts per serving: Calories 284.4, Total Fat 5.4 g, Carbs 34 g,*
*Protein 24.4 g, Sodium 1021.5 mg*

## Ingredients
Shrimp:
1 pound shrimp, peeled, deveined, and tail removed
Vegetable oil, as needed

Flour Mixture:
½ cup wheat flour
¼ teaspoon salt
1 teaspoon ground black pepper
1 teaspoon granulated garlic
½ teaspoon paprika
1 teaspoon granulated sugar

Eggs:
2 eggs, beaten

Breading:
1 cup breadcrumbs
1 teaspoon ground black pepper

## Preparation

1. Heat 3 inches of oil to 350°F.
2. Place the ingredients for the flour mixture in a bowl and mix. In separate bowls, beat the eggs and mix the breading ingredients together.
3. Dip the eggs in the flour mixture, then the eggs, then the breading.
4. After dipping, place the shrimp directly into the heated oil and cook for 2 to 3 minutes.
5. Place the cooked shrimp on a serving plate and serve with ketchup or tartar sauce.

# Disney World's Fulton's Crab House's Dungeness Crab Cakes

Disney World has amazing dishes—but you have to *enter* Disney World to eat them. So how about just making them in your kitchen?

*Serves: 4 – Preparation Time: 15 minutes – Cooking Time: 40 minutes*
*Nutrition facts per serving: Calories 200, Total Fat 6 g, Carbs 18 g,*
*Protein 18 g, Sodium 502 mg*

## *Ingredients*
2½ pounds Dungeness crabmeat
1⅛ cups unsalted soda crackers, crushed
⅛ cup Dijon mustard
½ teaspoon Old Bay Seasoning
⅛ cup mayonnaise
1 egg
3 tablespoons butter, melted

1-2 lemon, cut into thin wedges for serving
Bearnaise sauce for serving, if desired

## *Preparation*

1. To get started:
   a) Squeeze the crab meat to remove moisture;
   b) Preheat the oven to 425°F; and
   c) Butter a baking sheet.
2. Mix the mustard, seasoning, mayonnaise, and egg in a bowl. Refrigerate for 10 minutes.
3. Remove the mixture from the refrigerator, and add in the cracker crumbs. Continue mixing.
4. Pour the mixture over the crab and continue mixing.
5. Divide the mixture into 12, and then shape each dollop into a 1-inch thick circle.
6. Place the cakes on the baking sheet and drizzle some butter over each.
7. Bake for 15 to 20 minutes, until cakes are cooked through. Serve with lemon wedges and bearnaise sauce, if desired.

# Cheesecake Factory's Bang Bang Chicken and Shrimp

Cheesecake Factory blends Asian spices with seafood in a magical combination. If you love this dish as much as we do, then here is the recipe you've been looking for.

*Serves: 4 – Preparation Time: 10 minutes – Cooking Time: 50 minutes*
*Nutrition facts per serving: Calories 1211, Total Fat 84.2 g, Carbs 101 g,*
*Protein 30 g, Sodium 1940 mg*

## Ingredients

<u>Curry Sauce:</u>
2 teaspoons chili oil
¼ cup onion
2 tablespoons garlic cloves, minced
2 teaspoons ginger
1 cup chicken broth
½ teaspoon cumin, ground
½ teaspoon coriander, ground
½ teaspoon paprika
¼ teaspoon salt
¼ teaspoon black pepper, ground
¼ teaspoon mace, ground
¼ teaspoon turmeric
3 cups coconut milk
2 medium carrots, julienned
1 small zucchini, julienned
½ cup peas, frozen

<u>Peanut Sauce:</u>
¼ cup creamy peanut butter
2 tablespoons water
4 teaspoons sugar
1 tablespoon soy sauce
1 teaspoon rice vinegar
1 teaspoon lime juice
½ teaspoon chili oil

<u>Protein:</u>
2 chicken breast fillets, cut into bite-sized pieces
16 large shrimp, raw, shelled
¼ cup cornstarch
½ cup vegetable oil

<u>Final Dish:</u>
1½ cups flaked coconut
4 cups white rice, cooked
½ teaspoon dried parsley, crumbled
2 tablespoons peanuts, finely chopped
2 green onions, julienned

## *Preparation*

1. Sauté the onion, garlic, and ginger in heated chili oil for 30 seconds before adding in the broth.
2. Cook the mixture for another 30 seconds and then add in the cumin, coriander, paprika, salt, pepper, mace and turmeric.
3. Stir everything together and bring to a simmer. Keep the mixture at a simmer for 5 minutes and then add the coconut milk.
4. After adding the coconut milk, bring the mixture to a boil for 20 seconds.
5. Reduce the heat and then allow the mixture to simmer for 20 minutes before adding the carrots, zucchini, and peas.
6. Simmer the entire mixture for another 20 minutes and set the curry sauce aside. While waiting for the mixture to thicken, preheat the oven to 300°F.
7. Next, prepare the peanut sauce by mixing all of the ingredients together over medium heat.
8. When the peanut sauce starts to bubble, cover the pot, remove from heat, and set aside.
9. Spread the flaked coconut on a baking pan and bake for 30 minutes to toast. Swirl the flakes every 10 minutes, making sure they do not burn.
10. Pour the cornstarch in a bowl. Place the prepared chicken and shrimp into the bowl and cover entirely.
11. Sauté the chicken in the vegetable oil until it is cooked. Add the shrimp to the chicken and continue cooking.
12. Transfer the protein to a plate and set aside.

13. Arrange the dish as follows:
    a) Place some rice in the center of a plate;
    b) Place the chicken and shrimp around the rice;
    c) Pour the curry sauce over the chicken and the shrimp;
    d) Drizzle the peanut sauce over everything—especially the rice;
    e) Sprinkle some parsley and peanuts over the top of the rice, then top with the onions; then
    f) Sprinkle the toasted coconut flakes over the dish.
14. Serve and enjoy.

# Bubba Gump Shrimp Company's Cajun Shrimp

Cajun shrimp is a unique dish. If you love Bubba Gump's version, then try making this at home. It hits all the spots just right.

*Serves: 4 – Preparation Time: 5 minutes – Cooking Time: 15 minutes*
*Nutrition facts per serving: Calories 270, Total Fat 234 g, Carbs 169 g,*
*Protein 70 g, Sodium 2878 mg*

**Ingredients**
2 teaspoons paprika
1 teaspoon dried thyme
½ teaspoon salt
¼ teaspoon nutmeg, ground
¼ teaspoon garlic powder
⅛ teaspoon cayenne pepper

1 tablespoon olive oil
1 pound fresh medium-sized shrimp, peeled, deveined

## Preparation

1. Sauté all the ingredients (except for the shrimp) in oil for 30 seconds.
2. When the ingredients have heated up, add the shrimp and continue sautéing for 2 to 3 minutes.
3. When the shrimp is cooked entirely, transfer to a plate and serve.

# Olive Garden's Chicken and Shrimp Carbonara

Olive Garden places a delicious twist on the simple carbonara: They add shrimp and peppers that elevate pasta deliciousness. Here is the perfect recipe for you.

*Serves: 8 – Preparation Time: 35 minutes – Cooking Time: 40 minutes*
*Nutrition facts per serving: Calories 1570, Total Fat 113 g, Carbs 84 g,*
*Protein 55 g, Sodium 2400 mg*

### Ingredients

Shrimp Marinade

¼ cup extra virgin olive oil

½ cup water

2 teaspoons Italian seasoning

1 tablespoon minced garlic


Chicken

4 boneless and skinless chicken breasts cubed

1 egg mixed with 1 tablespoon cold water

½ cup panko bread crumbs

½ cup all-purpose flour

½ teaspoon salt

½ teaspoon black pepper

2 tablespoons olive oil


Carbonara sauce:

½ cup butter (1 stick)

3 tablespoons all-purpose flour

½ cup parmesan cheese, grated

2 cups heavy cream

2 cups milk

8 Canadian bacon slices, diced finely

¾ cup roasted red peppers, diced


Pasta

1 teaspoon salt

14 ounces spaghetti or bucatini pasta (1 package)

Water to cook the pasta


Shrimp

½ pound fresh medium shrimp, deveined and peeled

1-2 tablespoons olive oil for cooking

## Preparation

1. Mix all the marinade ingredients together in a re-sealable container or bag and add the add shrimp. Refrigerate for at least 30 minutes.

2. <u>To make the chicken</u>: Mix the flour, salt, pepper, and panko bread crumbs into a shallow dish. Whisk the egg with 1 tablespoon of cold water in a second shallow dish. Dip the chicken into the breadcrumb mix and after in the egg wash, and again in the breadcrumb mix. Place on a plate and let rest until all the chicken is prepared.

3. Warm the olive oil over medium heat in a deep large skillet. Working in batches, add the chicken. Cook for 4 to 6 minutes per side or until the chicken is cooked through. Place the cooked chicken tenders on a plate lined with paper towels to absorb excess oil.

4. <u>To make the pasta</u>: Add water to large pot and bring to a boil. Add salt and cook the pasta according to package instructions about 10-15 minutes before the sauce is ready.

5. To make the shrimp: While the pasta is cooking, add olive oil to a skillet. Remove the shrimp from the marinate and shake off the excess marinade. Cook the shrimp until they turn pink, about 2-3 minutes.

6. <u>To make the Carbonara sauce</u>: in a large deep skillet, sauté the Canadian bacon with a bit of butter for 3-4 minutes over medium heat or until the bacon starts to caramelize. Add the garlic and sauté for 1 more minute. Remove bacon and garlic and set aside.

7. In the same skillet, let the butter melt and mix-in the flour. Gradually add the cream and milk and whisk until the sauce thickens. Add the cheese.

8. Reduce the heat to a simmer and keep the mixture simmering while you prepare the rest of the ingredients.

9. When you are ready to serve, add the drained pasta, bacon bits, roasted red peppers to sauce. Stir to coat. Add pasta evenly to each serving plate. Top with some chicken and shrimp. Garnish with fresh parsley Serve with fresh shredded Romano or Parmesan cheese

# Copycat Vegetarian Recipes

## Olive Garden's Stuffed Mushrooms

If you're in a healthy mood, try Olive Garden's stuffed mushrooms. If you've already tried them, then here's how you make them at home.

*Serves: 6 – Preparation Time: 10 minutes – Cooking Time: 45 minutes*
*Nutrition facts per serving: Calories 293.1, Total Fat 20.3 g, Carbs 13.6 g,*
*Protein 14.7 g, Sodium 618.8 mg*

### Ingredients
Stuffed Mushrooms:
12 fresh mushrooms, washed, de-stemmed, and dried
1 teaspoon flat leaf parsley, minced
¼ teaspoon dry oregano
¼ cup + 1 tablespoon butter, divided; melted, cooled
¼ cup mozzarella cheese, finely grated
Some fresh parsley for garnish

<u>Stuffing:</u>
1 can (6 ounces) clams, drained, finely minced; save ¼ cup of juice
1 green onion, finely minced
1 egg, beaten
½ teaspoon garlic, minced
⅛ teaspoon garlic salt
½ cup Italian breadcrumbs
1 tablespoon red bell pepper, finely diced
2 tablespoons parmesan cheese, finely grated
1 tablespoon Romano cheese, finely grated
2 tablespoons mozzarella cheese, finely grated

## *Preparation*

1. Preheat the oven to 350°F and grease a small baking pan.
2. Thoroughly mix all the stuffing ingredients EXCEPT the clam juice and the cheeses.
3. When everything is blended, add in the clam juice and mix again. Next, add in the cheeses and continue mixing.
4. Stuff each of the mushrooms with about 1½ teaspoons of the mixture.
5. Pour 1 tablespoon of the butter into the baking pan and arrange the mushrooms on the pan. Then mix ¼ cup of the melted butter with the oregano and the parsley. Pour the butter mixture over the mushrooms.
6. Cover the pan with a lid or foil and bake for 35–40 minutes.
7. Uncover the mushrooms and sprinkle the remaining mozzarella cheese over the top. Bake for another few minutes, until the cheese melts.
8. Transfer to a serving plate. Garnish with parsley, if desired.

# P.F. Chang's Spicy Green Beans

Beans are amazing, but P.F. Chang was able to elevate the bean magic by adding spices and peppers. This healthy dish is bursting with flavor.

*Serves: 4 – Preparation Time: 10 minutes – Cooking Time: 10 minutes*
*Nutrition facts per serving: Calories 117.4, Total Fat 7.1 g, Carbs 12.4 g,*
*Protein 3.3 g, Sodium 511.1 mg*

## Ingredients

1 pound green beans, rinsed and trimmed
2 tablespoons fresh ginger, grated
2 tablespoons garlic, minced
2 tablespoons cooking oil
¼ cup water

Sauce:
2 tablespoons soy sauce
1 tablespoon rice vinegar
2 teaspoons sugar
2 tablespoons Szechuan peppercorn

## Preparation

1. Combine all the sauce ingredients in a bowl.
2. Bring some water to a boil and add the green beans. Cook for 3 to 5 minutes, or until crispy.
3. Sauté the garlic and ginger in the oil. When the mixture becomes aromatic, add in the green beans and cook for 2 to 3 minutes, or until soft
4. Add in the sauce and continue stirring the beans.
5. Serve with rice.

# Chili's Black Bean

Chili's has amazing bean dishes. If you love Chili's black beans as much as we do, then here is the answer to your prayers.

*Serves: 6 – Preparation Time: 5 minutes – Cooking Time: 25 minutes*
*Nutrition facts per serving: Calories 143.8, Total Fat 0.7 g, Carbs 25.9 g,*
*Protein 9.5.2 g, Sodium 5.5 mg*

### Ingredients
2 cans (15.5 ounces each) black beans
½ teaspoon sugar
1 teaspoon ground cumin
1 teaspoon chili powder
½ teaspoon garlic powder

2 tablespoon red onion, diced finely

½ teaspoon fresh cilantro, minced (optional)

½ cup water

Salt and black pepper to taste

Pico de Gallo and or sour cream for garnish *(optional)*

### Preparation

1. Combine the beans, sugar, cumin, chili powder, garlic, onion, cilantro (if using), and water in a saucepan and mix well.
2. Over medium-low heat, let the bean mixture simmer for about 20-25 minutes. Season with salt and pepper to taste.
3. Remove the beans from heat and transfer to serving bowls.
4. Garnish with Pico de Gallo and/or a dollop of sour cream, if desired.

# Same as In "N" Out'sAnimal Style Fries

When you need some comfort food and want to indulge, the Animal fries at In "N" Out can certainly satisfy your cravings. They are easy to make, luscious, and so, so, so good!

*Serves: 6-8 – Preparation Time: 10 minutes – Cooking Time: 30 minutes*
*Nutrition facts per serving: Calories 750, Total Fat 42 g, Carbs 54 g, Protein 19 g, Sodium 1105 mg*

## Ingredients
32 ounces frozen French fries
2 cups cheddar cheese, shredded
1 large onion, diced
2 tablespoons raw sugar
2 tablespoons olive oil
1 ½ cups mayonnaise
¾ cup ketchup

¼ cup sweet relish

1 ½ teaspoons white sugar

1 ½ teaspoons apple cider vinegar

½ teaspoon salt

½ teaspoon black pepper

## *Preparation*

1. Preheat oven to 350°F and place oven grill in the middle position.
2. Place fries on a large baking sheet and bake in the oven according package directions.
3. In the meantime, warm the olive oil in a large non-stick skillet over medium heat. Add the onions and sauté for about 2 minutes until fragrant and soft.
4. Add raw sugar and continue cooking until the onions caramelize. Remove from heat and set aside.
5. Add the mayonnaise, ketchup, relish, white sugar, salt and black pepper to a bowl and mix until well combined. Set aside.
6. Once the fries are cooked, remove from heat and set oven to broil.
7. Sprinkle with the cheddar cheese over the fries and place under the broiler until the cheese melts, about 2-3 minutes.
8. Add the cheese fries to serving bowls or plate. Add some caramelized onions on top and smother with mayonnaise sauce. Serve immediately.

# KFC's Coleslaw

While KFC is best known for their chicken, they also serve a mean coleslaw. We've found ourselves craving the vegetable dish more times that we can count. Here's how you can make it.

*Serves: 10 – Preparation Time: 15 minutes – Cooking Time: 0 minutes*
*Nutrition facts per serving: Calories 49.6, Total Fat 0.3 g, Carbs 11.3 g,*
*Protein 1.2 g, Sodium 138.3 mg*

### Ingredients
8 cups cabbage, *finely* diced
¼ cup carrot, *finely* diced
2 tablespoons onions, minced
⅓ cup granulated sugar

½ teaspoon salt
⅛ teaspoon pepper
¼ cup milk
½ cup mayonnaise
¼ cup buttermilk
1½ tablespoons white vinegar
2½ tablespoons lemon juice

## *Preparation*

1. Mix together the cabbage, carrot, and onions in a bowl.
2. Place the rest of the ingredients in a blender or food processor and blend until smooth. Pour the sauce over the cabbage mixture.
3. Place in the refrigerator for several hours before serving.

# Cracker Barrel's Baby Carrot

Some people argue that cooking the carrots in bacon grease negates the healthiness of the vegetable—but we don't particularly care; they're delicious!

*Serves: 6 – Preparation Time: 5 minutes – Cooking Time: 45 minutes*
*Nutrition facts per serving: Calories 205, Total Fat 8.6 g, Carbs 33.1 g,*
*Protein 1.1 g, Sodium 577.4 mg*

## Ingredients
1 teaspoon bacon grease, melted
2 pounds fresh baby carrots
Some water
1 teaspoon salt
¼ cup brown sugar
¼ cup butter, melted
¼ cup honey

## Preparation

1. Heat the bacon grease in a pot. Place the carrots in the grease and sauté for 10 seconds. Cover the carrots with water and add the salt.
2. Bring the entire mixture to a boil over medium heat, then reduce the heat to low and allow it to simmer for another 30 to 45 minutes. By this time, the carrots should be half cooked.
3. Remove half the water from the pot and add the rest of the ingredients.
4. Keep cooking until the carrots become tender. Transfer to a bowl and serve.

# Olive Garden's Gnocchi with Spicy Tomato and Wine Sauce

This simple but spicy pasta dish is both healthy and tasty. If you've tried Olive Garden's version, try this recipe for it.

*Serves: 4 – Preparation Time: 10 minutes – Cooking Time: 40 minutes*
*Nutrition facts per serving: Calories 285.8, Total Fat 18.9 g, Carbs 12.1 g,*
*Protein 8.4 g, Sodium 476.9 mg*

### *Ingredients*
Sauce:
2 tablespoons extra virgin olive oil
6 fresh garlic cloves
½ teaspoon chili flakes
1 cup dry white wine
1 cup chicken broth
2 cans (14.5 ounces each) tomatoes
¼ cup fresh basil, chopped

¼ cup sweet creamy butter, cut into 1-inch cubes, chilled
½ cup parmesan cheese, freshly grated

Pasta:
1 pound gnocchi
Salt, to taste
Black pepper, freshly crushed, to taste

**Preparation**

1. Place the olive oil, garlic and chili flakes in a cold pan and cook over medium heat.
2. When the garlic starts turning golden brown, add the wine and broth and bring the mixture to a simmer.
3. After about 10 minutes, the broth should be halved. When that happens, add in the tomatoes and basil and then let the sauce continue simmering for another 30 minutes.
4. Once the sauce has thickened, set it aside to cool for 3 minutes.
5. After 3 minutes, place the sauce in a blender, and add the butter and parmesan. Purée everything together and set aside.
6. Prepare the pasta by boiling the gnocchi in a large pot. When it is cooked, strain the pasta and mix with the sauce.
7. Transfer everything to a plate and serve.

# Melting Pot's Cheddar Cheese Fondue

If you're planning to serve some vegetables and fruits for dinner, here's a dip that will be a hit with the guests.

*Serves: 4 – Preparation Time: 15 minutes – Cooking Time: 15 minutes*
*Nutrition facts per serving: Calories 320, Total Fat 21 g, Carbs 7 g,*
*Protein 17 g, Sodium 473 mg*

## Ingredients

½ cup Coors Light beer

2 teaspoons garlic, chopped

2 teaspoons dry mustard powder

2 teaspoons Worcestershire sauce

6 ounces medium-sharp cheddar cheese, shredded or cubed

2 ounces Emmental Swiss cheese, shredded or cubed

2 tablespoons all-purpose flour

## Preparation

1. Place the beer, garlic, mustard powder and Worcestershire sauce in the top part of a double boiler and melt everything together.
2. Coat both cheeses with generous amounts of flour.
3. When the beer mixture is hot, slowly add in the cheese while mixing with a whisk.
4. When the cheese mixture becomes smooth, transfer it to a sauce plate and serve with chopped vegetables, bread, or fruits.

# Chipotle's Sofritas

This simple but healthy recipe is a great addition to your daily meals. Chipotle's special dish definitely looks beautiful on your table.

*Serves: 2 – Preparation Time: 10 minutes – Cooking Time: 25 minutes*
*Nutrition facts per serving: Calories 470, Total Fat 19 g, Carbs 59 g,*
*Protein 16 g, Sodium 1160 mg*

## Ingredients
Mexican Spice Mix:
½ teaspoon dried oregano leaves
2 teaspoons ancho chili powder, ground
1 teaspoon cumin, ground
½ teaspoon coriander, ground
½ teaspoon kosher salt

Sofritas:

1 tablespoon avocado or olive oil

½ medium onion, diced

2 garlic cloves, minced

1 teaspoon chipotle chili in adobo sauce, minced

1 tablespoon mild Hatch chili, diced

1 tablespoon Mexican Spice Mix

2 tablespoons tomato paste

1 package (16 ounces) organic extra firm tofu, drained, dried, crumbled

1 cup of your favorite Mexican beer

Salt and black pepper to taste

Tortillas and lime wedges for garnish

### Preparation

1. Place all the Mexican Spice Mix ingredients in a container or plastic bag and shake to mix.
2. Sauté the onion and garlic in oil over medium heat for 5 minutes.
3. Mix in both the chilies and the spice mix and sauté for another minute.
4. Pour in the tomato paste and cook for a minute.
5. Add the rest of the ingredients and cook for 5 more minutes. Taste and adjust seasoning with salt and pepper if required.
6. Remove the mixture from heat, transfer to a bowl, and then serve with tortillas and thin lime wedges.

# Copycat Burger and Sandwich Recipes

## Disneyland Blue Bayou's Monte Cristo Sandwich

This sandwich is special because of its rich flavors. If you're craving for a Monte Cristo sandwich but don't want to go all the way to Disneyland to get one, then here's how you can make it at home.

*Serves: 8 – Preparation Time: 10 minutes – Cooking Time: 5 minutes*
*Nutrition facts per serving: Calories 305, Total Fat 17.9 g, Carbs 23.7 g, Protein 12.2 g, Sodium 808 mg*

## Ingredients
1 quart oil

Sandwich:
8 slices white bread
4 slices turkey
4 slices ham
4 slices Swiss cheese
1 tablespoon confectioners' sugar

Batter:
⅔ cup water
1 egg
⅔ cup all-purpose flour
1¾ teaspoons baking powder
½ teaspoon salt
⅛ teaspoon black pepper, ground

## Preparation
1. Place 5 inches of oil over medium heat and bring to 365°F.
2. While the oil is heating, mix the wet and dry batter ingredients in two different bowls (i.e. egg and water; flour, baking powder, salt and pepper).
3. Slowly whisk the dry mixture into the egg mixture, then place the batter in the refrigerator.
4. Assemble the sandwiches in this order:
   a) Bottom bread;
   b) Turkey;
   c) Ham;
   d) Cheese;
   e) Ham; and
   f) Top bread.
5. Cut the sandwiches into four pieces and secure them with toothpicks. Remove the batter from the refrigerator.

6. Dip each sandwich in the batter, covering them completely, and immediately place in hot oil to deep fry.
7. When the batter turns golden brown, place the sandwiches on a plate and remove the toothpicks.
8. Dust the sandwiches with sugar and serve.

# In 'N' Out's Animal Style Burger

In 'N' Out burgers have been special since the dawn of time. Here's how you can make them right at home!

*Serves: 4 – Preparation Time: 15 minutes – Cooking Time: 40 minutes*
*Nutrition facts per serving: Calories 670, Total Fat 41 g, Carbs 39 g, Protein 37 g, Sodium 100 mg*

### Ingredients
<u>Caramelized Onions:</u>
2 tablespoons vegetable oil
2 large onions, finely chopped
¾ teaspoon kosher salt
½ cup water

Special Sauce:
¼ cup mayonnaise
2 tablespoons ketchup
1 tablespoon sweet pickle relish
½ teaspoon white vinegar

Burger:
2 pounds beef chuck, ground
4 hamburger buns
¼ cup dill pickles, sliced
¾ cup iceberg lettuce, shredded
4 to 8 thin slices tomato
Some freshly ground pepper
¼ cup yellow mustard
8 slices American cheese

## *Preparation*

1. Sauté the onions in the oil over medium heat. Season the onions with the salt.
2. Cover the pan, occasionally opening and stirring, until the onions turn golden brown.
3. After 30 minutes, uncover the pan and continue sautéing for another 8 minutes. Make sure that the onions caramelize.
4. Pour the water into the pan, bring the mixture to a simmer, and scrape off the burnt bits from the bottom. Keep cooking the onions until the water evaporates.
5. Transfer the onions to a bowl and set aside.
6. Mix the special sauce ingredients together in a bowl and set aside.
7. Divide the ground beef into 8 equal portions and shape them into patties. Season both sides with salt and pepper.
8. Toast the split-side of the hamburger buns on an oiled griddle.

9. Cook one side of the patties for 3 minutes. After 3 minutes, spread 1½ teaspoons of mustard on the uncooked side and flip. Place a slice of cheese on the flipped patty and cook for another 2 minutes.
10. Transfer the patties to a plate.
11. Assemble the burgers in this order:
    a) Bottom bun;
    b) 1 tablespoon of special sauce;
    c) Pickles;
    d) Lettuce;
    e) Tomato;
    f) Special sauce;
    g) Cooked patty with cheese;
    h) Caramelized onions;
    i) Cooked patty with cheese; and
    j) Top bun.
12. Place the burgers in foil for storage, or place on a plate and serve.

# Burger King's Big King Mushroom and Swiss Burger

Burger King is another famous burger joint. And this burger takes just 20 minutes to prepare!

*Serves: 4 – Preparation Time: 15 minutes – Cooking Time: 5 minutes*
*Nutrition facts per serving: Calories 444, Total Fat 22.2 g, Carbs 31.8 g,*
*Protein 28.4 g, Sodium 1451 mg*

## Ingredients
Mushroom Sauce:
1 can (10¾ ounces) condensed golden mushroom soup
1 can (4½ ounces) mushrooms, sliced, drained
1 teaspoon Worcestershire sauce

<u>Burger:</u>
1 ¼ pounds ground beef

1 teaspoon seasoned salt
½ teaspoon ground black pepper
6 hamburger buns
4 slices Swiss-style processed cheese

## *Preparation*
1. Mix the sauce ingredients in a saucepan and cook over low heat. Bring the mixture to a simmer, and continue to cook until step 4.
2. Season the beef with the rest of the ingredients (except the cheese), and divide into 8 equal portions. Shape the portions into patties, and don't forget to stir your mushrooms while you're doing it.
3. Heat a pan and cook the patties over medium heat for 3-5 minutes on each
4. When the patties are cooked, transfer them to a plate and remove the mushroom mixture from the heat. Assemble the burgers in this order:
   a) Bottom bun;
   b) Swiss cheese slice;
   c) Cooked patty;
   d) Middle bun;
   e) Second patty
   f) 1 to 2 tablespoons of mushroom sauce;
   g) Top bun.
5. Wrap the burgers in foil to store or place on a plate and serve.

# Manwich's Sloppy Joe

Both kids and adults absolutely *love* sloppy Joes. There's no way to eat them neatly!

*Serves: 4 – Preparation Time: 10 minutes – Cooking Time: 25 minutes*
*Nutrition facts per serving: Calories 323.4, Total Fat 17.4 g, Carbs 19.7 g,*
*Protein 23.2 g, Sodium 1644.4 mg*

## Ingredients
1 pound ground beef
1 can (8 ounces) tomato sauce
1 cup ketchup
1 tablespoon dried onion flakes
1 tablespoon green pepper, finely chopped
1 teaspoon salt
½ teaspoon garlic, minced
¼ teaspoon celery seed
½ teaspoon chili powder
1 teaspoon mustard

4 hamburger buns
Some cheese, shredded
Some pickles
Mustard

## *Preparation*

1. Sauté the ground beef in a pot until brown.
2. Drain the fat and then add the rest of the ingredients up to the hamburger buns to the pot.
3. Bring the entire mixture to a boil. When the mixture is boiling, lower the heat and allow it to simmer for another 10 minutes.
4. While the mixture is simmering, toast the hamburger buns.
5. Assemble the sloppy Joes in this order:
   a) Bottom bun;
   b) Pickles;
   c) Beef mixture;
   d) Mustard;
   e) Cheese; and
   f) Top bun.
6. Serve and enjoy.

# Burger King's Rodeo Burger

Here's another recipe that will satisfy your Burger King cravings. It has an extra crunch that was lacking in the other burger.

*Serves: 1 – Preparation Time: 5 minutes – Cooking Time: 20 minutes*
*Nutrition facts per serving: Calories 310, Total Fat 13 g, Carbs 38 g,*
*Protein 9 g, Sodium 450 mg*

## Ingredients
1 fully cooked hamburger patty
1 hamburger bun with sesame seeds
3-4 small onion rings, baked
2 slices pickles
2 tablespoons barbecue sauce

## Preparation

1. If making your patty at home, season some ground beef with salt and pepper and shape into a patty.
2. Fry the patty on both sides until it is fully cooked.
3. While the patty is frying, toast the buns.
4. Assemble the burger like this:
   a) Bottom bun;
   b) Meat patty;
   c) Onion rings;
   d) Pickles;
   e) Barbecue sauce; and
   f) Top bun.
5. Place the burger on a plate and enjoy.

# Shake Shack's Smoke Shack Burger

This item is a part of the Shake Shack's secret menu—some branches don't even have it! When you're missing that smoky burger, make it right at home.

*Serves: 4 – Preparation Time: 10 minutes – Cooking Time: 25 minutes*
*Nutrition facts per serving: Calories 620, Total Fat 42 g, Carbs 26 g,*
*Protein 35 g, Sodium 1602 mg*

## Ingredients
Sauce:
½ cup mayonnaise
1 tablespoon Dijon mustard
¾ teaspoon ketchup

¼ teaspoon kosher dill pickle juice
Pinch of cayenne pepper

Burger:
4 potato hamburger buns
¼ cup unsalted butter, melted
8 smoked bacon slices, cooked, halved
½ cup pickled red cherry peppers, diced
1 pound very cold ground beef (shaped into 4 (1-inch-thick) patties)
1 teaspoon kosher salt, divided
¼ teaspoon black pepper, divided
4 slices American cheese

## Preparation
1. Thoroughly mix all of the sauce ingredients together.
2. Butter the insides of the hamburger buns and toast on a hot griddle for 2 to 3 minutes.
3. Remove the buns and heat the griddle for another 2 to 3 minutes while seasoning one side of each patty with salt and pepper.
4. Place the patties on the heated griddle, with the seasoned side facing the griddle. Use a spatula to squish the patties to ⅓-inch thick.
5. Sprinkle the unseasoned side of the patties with salt and pepper and leave to cook for 2 to 3 minutes.
6. When the patty juices are bubbling, flip them and place the cheese slices on top.
7. When the bottom sides of the patties are charred, transfer them from the griddle to the bottom hamburger bun. You can put lettuce on the bun before the patty, if you like.
8. Place the cherry peppers and bacon on top of the cheese, and top everything off with the hamburger bun.
9. Secure the sandwich with a toothpick and serve.

# Copycat Pasta Recipes

## Olive Garden's Fettuccine Alfredo

Olive Garden's classic Fettuccine Alfredo is a simple yet elegant dish. It's easy to make and delicious to eat.

*Serves: 6 – Preparation Time: 5 minutes – Cooking Time: 25 minutes*
*Nutrition facts per serving: Calories 767.3, Total Fat 52.9 g, Carbs 57.4 g, Protein 17.2 g, Sodium 367 mg*

**Ingredients**
½ cup butter, melted
2 tablespoons cream cheese
1 pint heavy cream
1 teaspoon garlic powder
Some salt
Some black pepper
⅔ cup parmesan cheese, grated
1 pound fettuccine, cooked

## Preparation

1. Melt the cream cheese in the melted butter over medium heat until soft.
2. Add the heavy cream and season the mixture with garlic powder, salt, and pepper.
3. Reduce the heat to low and allow the mixture to simmer for another 15 to 20 minutes.
4. Remove the mixture from heat and add in the parmesan. Stir everything to melt the cheese.
5. Pour the sauce over the pasta and serve.

# Red Lobster's Shrimp Pasta

Seafood and pasta is always a beautiful combination. Make this at home and enjoy a special meal.

*Serves: 4 – Preparation Time: 5 minutes – Cooking Time: 30 minutes*
*Nutrition facts per serving: Calories 590, Total Fat 26 g, Carbs 54 g,*
*Protein 34 g, Sodium 1500 mg*

### Ingredients
8 ounces linguini or spaghetti pasta
⅓ cup extra virgin olive oil
3 garlic cloves
1 pound shrimp, peeled, deveined
⅔ cup clam juice or chicken broth
⅓ cup white wine
1 cup heavy cream
½ cup parmesan cheese, freshly grated
¼ teaspoon dried basil, crushed

¼ teaspoon dried oregano, crushed
Fresh parsley and parmesan cheese for garnish

## *Preparation*

1. Cook the Pasta according to package directions.
2. Simmer the garlic in hot oil over low heat, until tender.
3. Increase the heat to low to medium and add the shrimp. When the shrimp is cooked, transfer it to a separate bowl along with the garlic. Keep the remaining oil in the pan.
4. Pour the clam or chicken broth into the pan and bring to a boil.
5. Add the wine and adjust the heat to medium. Keep cooking the mixture for another 3 minutes.
6. While stirring the mixture, reduce the heat to low and add in the cream and cheese. Keep stirring.
7. When the mixture thickens, return the shrimp to the pan and throw in the remaining ingredients (except the pasta).
8. Place the pasta in a bowl and pour the sauce over it.
9. Mix everything together and serve. Garnish with parsley and parmesan cheese, if desired

# Noodles and Company's Indonesian Peanut Sauté

This delicious Thai dish has just enough kick to make your taste buds happy. Make this Noodles and Company recipe right in your kitchen!

*Serves: 4 – Preparation Time: 5 minutes – Cooking Time: 30 minutes*
*Nutrition facts per serving: Calories 940, Total Fat 21 g, Carbs 148 g,*
*Protein 41 g, Sodium 2400 mg*

## Ingredients
<u>Marinade</u>
1 tablespoon hot sauce, like Sriracha
Juice of 1 lime
3 cloves garlic, pressed
1 tablespoon fresh ginger, minced
2 teaspoons soy sauce
Salt & pepper, to taste

Other ingredients
Vegetable oil
2 pounds boneless, skinless chicken, cut into thin strips
1 package (16-ounces) linguine noodles
½ cup shoestring carrots
½ cup broccoli florets
4-5 green onions, diced finely
1 cup bean sprouts, plus some more for garnish
Some peanuts, crushed for garnish
Fresh cilantro for garnish
2–3 limes, cut into wedges for garnish

<u>Peanut Sauce</u>
1 cup chicken broth
6 tablespoons creamy peanut butter
2–4 teaspoons Sriracha chili sauce, depending on how hot you like it
3 tablespoons honey
6 tablespoons soy sauce
3 tablespoons fresh minced ginger
4–5 cloves garlic, pressed or minced

### Preparation

1. Mix the marinade ingredients together in a bowl. Add the chicken and let soak 10-15 minutes. Remove chicken and
2. Warm 1-2 tablespoons of vegetable oil in a large sauté pan such as a wok. Sauté the chicken in the Sriracha mixture.
3. Cook the pasta al dente according to package directions. Remove the chicken from heat and wrap it in foil to retain its warmth.
4. While waiting for the pasta to cook, make the peanut sauce by mixing all the ingredients in a small saucepan over medium to low heat. Keep cooking and stirring the sauce until it becomes smooth, about 3 minutes.
5. Using the pan you used to cook the chicken, sauté the vegetables in oil. Add the beansprouts last so that they do not get overcooked.
6. When the beansprouts are half cooked, mix in the warm chicken and cover the pan. Lower the heat.
7. When the noodles are cooked, drain them from the water and transfer them to the sauté pan. Add the peanut sauce and stir to coat.
8. To serve, divide into four bowls. Garnish with cilantro, crushed peanuts, and bean sprouts.

# Cheesecake Factory's Cajun Jambalaya Pasta

If the last seafood pasta wasn't quite what you were looking for, here is another one that you may like even more.

*Serves: 4 – Preparation Time: 10 minutes – Cooking Time: 40 minutes*
*Nutrition facts per serving: Calories 563.9, Total Fat 13.3 g, Carbs 73.8 g, Protein 35.9 g, Sodium 1457.6 mg*

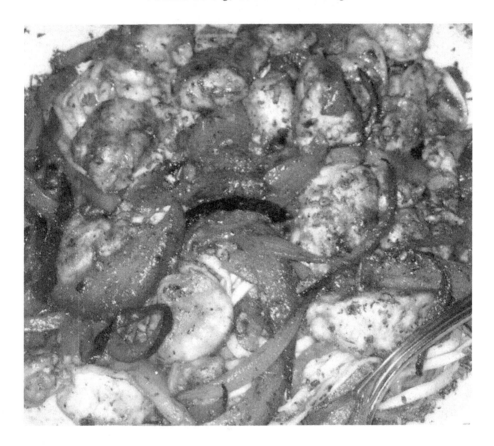

## Ingredients
Cajun Seasoning Blend:
1 teaspoon white pepper
1 teaspoon cayenne pepper
3 teaspoons salt

1 teaspoon paprika
½ teaspoon garlic powder
½ teaspoon onion powder

Chicken and Shrimp:
2 boneless skinless chicken breasts, halved, cut into bite-size
pieces
½ pound large shrimp, peeled, deveined
1 tablespoon olive oil

Pasta:
5 quarts water
6 ounces fettuccine
6 ounces spinach fettuccine

Jambalaya:
1 tablespoon olive oil
2 medium tomatoes, chopped
1 medium onion, sliced
1 green bell pepper, sliced
1 red bell pepper, sliced
1 yellow bell pepper, sliced
1½ cups chicken stock
1 tablespoon cornstarch
2 tablespoons white wine
2 teaspoons arrowroot powder
2 teaspoons fresh parsley, chopped

## Preparation

1. Mix all of the Cajun seasoning blend ingredients together to make the seasoning. Divide the seasoning into 3 equal parts.
2. Coat the chicken and shrimp with ⅓ of the seasoning each.
3. Cook pasta according to package directions.

4. While waiting for the pasta, sauté the spiced chicken in heated oil in a large skillet.
5. When the chicken starts turning brown, stir in the shrimp and cook until the chicken is cooked though and shrimp turn pink.
6. Transfer the chicken and shrimp to a plate and set aside.
7. Using the same pan, warm the oil for the jambalaya over medium heat. Add the tomatoes, onions, peppers, and remaining 1/3 of the seasoning mix. Sauté for 10 minutes.
8. When the vegetables turn brownish-black, add the chicken and shrimp back to the mix.
9. Pour in ¾ cup of the chicken stock to deglaze the pan. Gently scrape the pan to remove the burnt particles. Turn the heat to high and allow the mixture to cook.
10. When the broth has evaporated completely, add in the remaining stock and cook for another 5 minutes.
11. Turn the heat down to low and leave the mixture to rest over heat. In a bowl, mix the white wine and arrowroot until it dissolves.
12. Add the mixture to the jambalaya. Turn the heat to low and leave the mixture to simmer.
13. When the jambalaya and pasta are done, assemble the dish by:
    a) Putting the pasta as the first layer;
    b) Covering the pasta with the jambalaya sauce; and
    c) Garnish each plate with parsley.

# Noodles and Company's Pad Thai

If you need some comfort food, why not make yourself a Pad Thai? This dish is refreshing and delicious.

*Serves: 4 – Preparation Time: 5 minutes – Cooking Time: 20 minutes*
*Nutrition facts per serving: Calories 830, Total Fat 18 g, Carbs 151 g,*
*Protein 15 g, Sodium 1300 mg*

### *Ingredients*
Sauce:
½ cup boiling water
¼ cup brown sugar
6 tablespoons lime juice
¼ cup rice vinegar
¼ cup Thai fish sauce
2 teaspoons Sriracha

Pad Thai:

12 ounces fettuccine or linguine (uncooked)
2 tablespoons canola oil, divided
½ yellow onion, sliced
3 cloves fresh garlic. pressed or minced
3 eggs, lightly beaten
½ cup cabbage, sliced
½ cup mushrooms, sliced
1 cup carrots, sliced
1 cup broccoli, chopped
Garnish: cilantro, sliced green onions, lime wedges

***Preparation***

1. Dissolve the sugar in the boiling water. When the sugar has completely dissolved, mix in the lime juice, vinegar, fish sauce, and Sriracha.
2. Cook the noodles.
3. Sauté the onion in 1 tablespoon of oil over medium to high heat for 1 minute. Add in the garlic and sauté for another 30 seconds. Mix the eggs into the garlic and onion mixture, and continue to cook until the egg is cooked completely.
4. Transfer the egg mixture to a bowl and add the remaining oil to the same pan. Sauté the vegetables.
5. When the vegetables are crispy, add in half of the sauce and cook for 1 to 3 minutes. When your desired consistency is reached, add in the egg mixture and noodles and transfer to a plate to serve.

# Cheesecake Factory's Pasta di Vinci

Nothing is as perfect as pasta with mushrooms. Here's Cheesecake Factory's Pasta Di Vinci—make and eat as much as you like.

*Serves: 4 – Preparation Time: 10 minutes – Cooking Time: 50 minutes*
*Nutrition facts per serving: Calories 844.9, Total Fat 35.8 g, Carbs 96.5 g,*
*Protein 33.9 g, Sodium 1400.2 mg*

## Ingredients
½ red onion, chopped
1 cup mushrooms, quartered
2 teaspoons garlic, chopped
1 pound chicken breast, cut into bite-size pieces
3 tablespoons butter, divided
2 tablespoons flour
2 teaspoons salt
¼ cup white wine
1 cup cream of chicken soup mixed with some milk
4 tablespoons heavy cream
Basil leaves for serving, chopped

Parmesan cheese for serving

1 pound penne pasta, cooked, drained

## Preparation

1. Sauté the onion, mushrooms and garlic in 1 tablespoon of the butter.
2. When they are tender, remove them from the butter and place in a bowl. Cook the chicken in the same pan.
3. When the chicken is done, transfer it to the bowl containing the garlic, onions, and mushrooms, and set everything aside.
4. Using the same pan, make a roux using the flour and remaining butter over low to medium heat. When the roux is ready, mix in the salt, wine, and cream of chicken mixture. Continue stirring the mixture, making sure that it does not burn.
5. When the mixture thickens and allow the mixture to simmer for a few more minutes.
6. Mix in the ingredients that you set aside, and transfer the cooked pasta to a bowl or plate.
7. Pour the sauce over the pasta, garnish with parmesan cheese and basil, and serve.

# Longhorn Steakhouse's Mac & Cheese

Mac & cheese is a classic American dish. Longhorn Steakhouse's Mac and Cheese is to die for. If you don't believe us, make some and try it.

*Serves: 10 – Preparation Time: 20 minutes – Cooking Time: 20 minutes*
*Nutrition facts per serving: Calories 610, Total Fat 37 g, Carbs 43 g,*
*Protein 26 g, Sodium 1210 mg*

## Ingredients
1 pound cavatappi pasta, cooked
2 tablespoons butter
2 tablespoons flour

2 cups half-and-half
2 ounces gruyere cheese, shredded
8 ounces white cheddar, shredded
2 tablespoons parmesan cheese, shredded
4 ounces fontina cheese, shredded
1 teaspoon smoked paprika
4 pieces bacon, crispy, crumbled
½ cup panko bread crumbs

## Preparation

1. Make a roux by cooking the melted butter and flour over medium heat.
2. When the roux is cooked, add in the half-and-half ½ cup at a time, adding more as the sauce thickens.
3. Slowly add the rest of the ingredients (except the pasta) one at a time, really allowing each ingredient to incorporate itself into the sauce. Continue stirring the mixture until everything is heated.
4. Place the pasta in a greased 13×9 baking pan or 6 individual baking dishes and pour the sauce over it. Sprinkle the bacon and panko bread crumbs over the top of the pasta.
5. Bake the pasta in an oven preheated to 350°F for 20-25 minutes, or until breadcrumbs start to become golden brown.
6. Let the pasta cool, and serve.

# Fazoli's Baked Garlic Chicken Spaghetti

Fazoli has a great spaghetti recipe—and here it is. If you want some pasta, this recipe is a great dish just for you.

*Serves: 8 – Preparation Time: 15 minutes – Cooking Time: 45 minutes*
*Nutrition facts per serving: Calories 350, Total Fat 7 g, Carbs 43 g,*
*Protein 11 g, Sodium 430 mg*

## Ingredients
Batter:
½ cup biscuit mix
2 tablespoons parmesan cheese, grated
1 teaspoon basil
1 teaspoon oregano
½ teaspoon garlic powder
¼ teaspoon pepper

Chicken:
2 tablespoons olive oil, divided
4 boneless chicken breast halves
1 cup mozzarella cheese

Pasta:
1 quart homemade tomato sauce
1 can (28 ounces) spaghetti sauce
3–5 garlic cloves, minced
3 cups mozzarella cheese, shredded
12 ounces linguine, cooked, drained
½ cup parmesan cheese

## Preparation

1. To get started:
   a) Preheat the oven to 350°F;
   b) Preheat a pan over medium to high heat; and
   c) Oil a 13×9 baking pan with 1 tablespoon of olive oil
2. Mix all of the batter ingredients together thoroughly. Dip the chicken breasts into the batter, covering each completely.
3. Place the remaining olive oil into a pan and brown the chicken on each side.
4. Mix the tomato sauce, spaghetti sauce and garlic in a separate bowl.
5. Cover the bottom of the pan with ⅓ of the pasta. Spread ¼ of the cheese over the pasta as the second layer. Spread 1 cup of the sauce over the second layer.
6. Repeat step 5 until all you have left is a little sauce. Keep 1 cup of mozzarella cheese for the chicken
7. Place the chicken on top of everything and cover with the remaining sauce.
8. Bake the pasta for 30 minutes, then top with remaining mozzarella cheese..
9. Bake for another 10 minutes, slice, and serve.

# Sbarro's Baked Ziti

No need to go to Sbarro's to get your pasta fix. Make it right at home and enjoy it however you like!

*Serves: 8-10 – Preparation Time: 5 minutes – Cooking Time: 40 minutes*
*Nutrition facts per serving: Calories 840, Total Fat 31 g, Carbs 101 g,*
*Protein 40 g, Sodium 1250 mg*

### Ingredients
2 pounds ziti pasta, cooked, drained
1½ pounds mozzarella cheese, shredded
1 cup roasted garlic-and-onion spaghetti sauce
Cooking spray
Garlic bread to serve

<u>Pasta Sauce:</u>

2 pounds ricotta cheese

3 ounces Romano cheese, grated

3 cups roasted garlic-and-onion spaghetti sauce

½ teaspoon black pepper

## *Preparation*

1. Get started by:
    a) Preheating the oven to 350°F;
    b) Cooking and draining the pasta according to package instructions; and
    c) Lightly coat a 13×9 baking pan with cooking spray.
2. Thoroughly mix together the pasta sauce ingredients.
3. Combine the pasta sauce with the cooked ziti.
4. Spread the spaghetti sauce over the bottom of the baking pan.
5. Add the ziti atop the sauce and sprinkle everything with the mozzarella cheese.
6. Loosely cover the pasta with aluminum foil and bake for 12 to 15 minutes, or until the cheese is well melted and the edges of the pan are bubbly and golden.
7. You can also, set the oven to broil, uncover the ziti and set under the broiler for 1-2 minutes until the cheese is golden (optional).
8. Transfer to a plate and serve with garlic bread.

# Olive Garden's Steak Gorgonzola

Steak gorgonzola is always delicious. But Olive Garden's pasta brings deliciousness to a whole new level. Make this simple dish at home and enjoy over a few days.

*Serves: 6 – Preparation Time: 10 minutes – Cooking Time: 1 hour 30 minutes*
*Nutrition facts per serving: Calories 740.5, Total Fat 27.7 g, Carbs 66 g,*
*Protein 54.3 g, Sodium 848.1 mg*

**Ingredients**
Pasta:
2½ pounds boneless beef top sirloin steaks, cut into ½-inch cubes
1 pound fettucine or linguini, cooked
2 tablespoons sun-dried tomatoes, chopped
2 tablespoons balsamic vinegar glaze
Some fresh parsley leaves, chopped

<u>Marinade:</u>
1½ cups Italian dressing
1 tablespoon fresh rosemary, chopped
1 tablespoon fresh lemon juice *(optional)*

<u>Spinach Gorgonzola Sauce:</u>
4 cups baby spinach, trimmed
2 cups Alfredo sauce (recipe follows)
½ cup green onion, chopped
6 tablespoons gorgonzola, crumbled, and divided)

**Preparation**
1. Cook the pasta and set aside. Mix together the marinade ingredients in a sealable container.
2. Marinate the beef in the container for an hour.
3. While the beef is marinating, make the Spinach Gorgonzola sauce. Heat the Alfredo sauce in a saucepan over medium heat. Add spinach and green onions. Let simmer until the spinach wilt. Crumble 4 tablespoons of the Gorgonzola cheese on top of the sauce. Let melt and stir. Set aside remaining 2 tablespoons of the cheese for garnish. Set aside and cover with lid to keep warm.
4. When the beef is done marinating, grill each piece depending on your preference.
5. Toss the cooked pasta and the Alfredo sauce in a saucepan, and then transfer to a plate.
6. Top the pasta with the beef, and garnish with balsamic glaze, sun-dried tomatoes, crumble gorgonzola cheese, and parsley leaves.
7. Serve and enjoy.

# Olive Garden's Copycat Alfredo Sauce

*Serves 4-6 - Preparation Time: 10 minutes - Cooking Time: 10 minutes*

## Ingredients
6 tablespoons butter (1 ½ sticks)
1 tablespoon garlic, minced
2 tablespoons all-purpose flour
1 ½ cups milk
1 ½ cups heavy cream
½ cup Parmesan cheese, grated
½ cup Romano cheese, grated
Salt and white pepper

## Preparation
1. In a large saucepan, let the butter melt over medium heat. Add the garlic and stir for about a minute.
2. Add the flour and stir until you have a soft paste. Gradually add the milk and the cream. Increase the heat to medium high until the sauce start to bubble and lower the heat to medium again. Stir in the cheeses. Continue whisking continuously until you get the desired consistency. Season to taste with salt and pepper.
3. Remove from heat. Serve over your favorite pasta.

# Copycat Dessert Recipes

## Panera Bread's Chocolate Chip Cookies

Do you want a special chocolate chip cookie for dessert? Here is the recipe for Panera Bread's cookies.

*Serves: 12 – Preparation Time: 15 minutes – Cooking Time: 15 minutes*
*Nutrition facts per serving: Calories 440, Total Fat 23 g,*
*Carbs 59 g, Protein 4 g, Sodium 240 mg*

### Ingredients
2½ sticks unsalted butter
1¼ cup dark brown sugar
¼ cup granulated sugar
2 teaspoons vanilla extract
2 eggs
3½ cups all-purpose flour
1 tablespoon cornstarch
1 teaspoon baking soda

1 teaspoon salt
1 bag (12 ounces) mini semisweet chocolate chips

## Preparation

1. Cream the butter and sugars using a whisk or a hand mixer.
2. Whip in the vanilla extract and eggs and set the wet mixture aside.
3. In a different bowl, mix together the flour, cornstarch, baking soda, and salt.
4. Pour the dry mixture into the wet mixture a little at a time, folding with a spatula. Add in the chocolate chips and continue folding.
5. Roll the cookie dough into balls and place them on a baking sheet. Place the baking sheet in the freezer for 15 minutes.
6. Preheat the oven to 350°F while waiting for the cookies to harden.
7. Transfer the cookies from the freezer to the oven immediately and bake for 15 minutes.

# Tommy Bahama's Key Lime Pie

This refreshing dessert is the perfect end to a meal. Make some for family and friends for happy taste buds.

*Serves: 2 – Preparation Time: 40 minutes – Cooking Time: 50 minutes*
*Nutrition facts per serving: Calories 500, Total Fat 9 g, Carbs 26 g,*
*Protein 1 g, Sodium 110 mg*

## *Ingredients*
Pie:
10-inch graham cracker crust
1 egg white
2½ cups sweetened condensed milk
¾ cup pasteurized egg yolk
1 cup lime juice
1 lime, zest
1 lime, sliced into 8

<u>White Chocolate Mousse Whipped Cream:</u>
8 fluid ounces heavy cream
3 tablespoons powdered sugar
¼ teaspoon pure vanilla extract
½ tablespoon white chocolate mousse instant mix

## *Preparation*

1. Preheat the oven to 350°F while brushing the graham cracker crust with the egg white. Cover the crust completely before placing it in the oven to bake for 5 minutes.
2. Whip the egg yolk and condensed milk together until they are blended completely. Add the lime juice and zest to the mixture and continue whipping until the mixture is smooth.
3. If you haven't yet, remove the crust from the oven and let it cool. When the crust has cooled, add in the egg mixture and bake at 250°F for 25 to 30 minutes.
4. When the pie is cooked, place it on a cooling rack to cool. Then place it in the refrigerator for at least two hours.
5. While waiting for the pie to cool, beat the first three whipped cream ingredients for two minutes (if using a hand mixer). When the mixture is smooth, add in the chocolate mousse and beat to stiff peaks.
6. Remove the pie from the refrigerator, slice it into eight pieces, and garnish each with the white chocolate mousse whipped cream and a slice of lime. Serve.

# Dairy Queen's Blizzard

Dairy Queen's ice cream always hits the spot. If you're craving a Blizzard but there's no DQ in your neighborhood, here's an easy recipe that will satisfy your cravings.

*Serves: 1 – Preparation Time: 5 minutes – Cooking Time: 0 minutes*
*Nutrition facts per serving: Calories 953, Total Fat 51.6 g, Carbs 108.8 g,*
*Protein 15.1 g, Sodium 439.4 mg*

### Ingredients

1 candy bar, of your choice
¼ to ½ cup milk
2½ cups vanilla ice cream
1 teaspoon fudge sauce

### Preparation

1. Place the candy bar of your choice into the freezer to harden it.
2. Break the candy bar into multiple tiny chunks and place all the ingredients into a blender.
3. Keep blending until the ice cream becomes thicker and everything is mixed completely.
4. Pour into a cup and consume.

# Olive Garden's Tiramisu

This classic Italian dessert can make an ordinary meal extraordinary. If you don't know what dessert to serve, try out Olive Garden's tiramisu—you won't regret it.

*Serves: 9 – Preparation Time: 10 minutes – Cooking Time: 2 hours 40 min.*
*Nutrition facts per serving: Calories 288.6, Total Fat 14 g, Carbs 34.4 g,*
*Protein 4.4 g, Sodium 53.6 mg*

**Ingredients**
4 egg yolks
2 tablespoons milk
⅔ cup granulated sugar
2 cups mascarpone cheese
¼ teaspoon vanilla extract
1 cup heavy cream
½ cup cold espresso
¼ cup Kahlua

20–24 ladyfingers

2 teaspoons cocoa powder

### Preparation

1. Bring water to a boil, then reduce the heat to maintain a simmer. Place a heatproof bowl over the water, making sure that the bowl does not touch the water.
2. In the heatproof bowl, whisk together the egg yolks, milk and sugar for about 8 to 10 minutes.
3. When the mixture has thickened, remove the bowl from heat and then whisk in the vanilla and mascarpone cheese until the mixture becomes smooth.
4. In another bowl, whisk the cream until soft peaks are formed.
5. Using a spatula, fold the whipped cream into the mascarpone mixture, making sure to retain the fluffiness of the whipped cream.
6. In another bowl, mix the espresso and Kahlua.
7. Dip the ladyfingers into the espresso mixture one by one. Dip only the bottom, and dip them quickly so as not to make them soggy.
8. Cover the bottom of an 8×8 pan with half of the dipped ladyfingers, cracking them if necessary.
9. Pour half of the mascarpone mixture over the ladyfingers.
10. Place another layer of ladyfingers over the mixture.
11. Pour the rest of the mixture over the second layer of ladyfingers and smooth out the top.
12. Dust some cocoa powder over the top and then place in the refrigerator.
13. Slice the cake and serve when set.

# Cheesecake Factory's Oreo Cheesecake

Anything with Oreo is already a must-try. But Cheesecake Factory's Oreo Cheesecake—it's to die for. Have this simple cake at the end of your meal as a treat for your taste buds.

*Serves: 10 – Preparation Time: 25 minutes – Cooking Time: 1 hour*
*Nutrition facts per serving: Calories 1520, Total Fat 55 g, Carbs 175 g, Protein 0 g, Sodium 736 mg*

## *Ingredients*
Crust:
1½ cups Oreo cookies, crushed
2 tablespoons butter, melted

Filling:
3 packages (8 ounces each) cream cheese, room temperature
1 cup sugar
5 large eggs, room temperature

2 teaspoons vanilla extract

¼ teaspoon salt

¼ cup all-purpose flour

1 container (8 ounces) sour cream, room temperature

14 Oreo cookies, divided

### Preparation

1. To make the crust, crush whole Oreos in a blender or smash them with a rolling pin and mix them with the melted butter. Press the Oreo mixture to the bottom and sides of a 9-inch spring form pan.
2. Leave the crust to rest and preheat the oven to 325°F. Before starting to make the filling, make sure all of your ingredients are at room temperature.
3. Place the cream cheese in a medium-sized bowl and beat it with a hand mixer or a whisk until it is light and fluffy.
4. Beat in the sugar, mixing continuously so that the sugar is evenly distributed throughout the mixture.
5. Beat in the eggs, one at a time, and then add in the vanilla, salt, and flour. When the ingredients are all mixed together, add in the sour cream and 6 chopped Oreos.
6. Pour the filling onto the crust and then top with 8 whole Oreos.
7. Bake in the oven for an hour to an hour and 15 minutes. When the cake is done baking, leave it in the oven with the door open for an hour.
8. When it has cooled down, transfer the cake to the refrigerator. Leave it for a day or more before serving.

# TCBY's Chocolate Yogurt Pie

If you miss TCBY's healthy pies but don't want to leave your house, here's how you can stay in your humble abode while satisfying your cravings.

*Serves: 2 – Preparation Time: 10 minutes – Cooking Time: 8 hours 30 min.*
*Nutrition facts per serving: Calories 330, Total Fat 13 g, Carbs 49 g,*
*Protein 4 g, Sodium 160 mg*

## Ingredients
⅔ cup butter
1¼ cups sugar
1 cup unsweetened cocoa powder

¼ teaspoon salt
½ teaspoon vanilla extract
2 large eggs
½ cup all-purpose flour
1 pint TCBY chocolate yogurt
Whipped cream
Caramel syrup

## Preparation

1. Before you begin, preheat the oven to 325°F.
2. Place a heatproof bowl in simmering water and mix the butter, sugar, cocoa powder and salt over the heat.
3. Continue stirring and heating the mixture until it becomes smooth. Remove the bowl from the heat and set aside.
4. When the mixture becomes a little cooler, mix in the vanilla extract and the eggs, one at a time. Make sure that the mixture is not too hot so that the eggs do not get cooked.
5. Beat the flour into the mixture with a wooden spoon until the entire mixture is thoroughly blended.
6. Transfer the mixture to a greased baking pan and then bake for 20 to 25 minutes.
7. Remove the pie from the oven and transfer to a cooling rack.
8. When the pie has cooled down, spread frozen yogurt over the surface and freeze for 10 to 15 minutes.
9. Garnish the yogurt pie with whipped cream and caramel syrup, and then return to the freezer for at least 8 hours.
10. Cut the pie into equal portions and serve.

# P.F. Chang's Ginger Panna Cotta

If you need to clean your palate after a heavy meal, here is a dessert that will refresh your taste buds. Thank you, P.F. Chang, for this wonderful treat.

*Serves: 3 – Preparation Time: 10 minutes – Cooking Time: 4 hours 10 min.*
*Nutrition facts per serving: Calories 346, Total Fat 30 g, Carbs 16 g,*
*Protein 4 g, Sodium 50 mg*

### *Ingredients*
Panna Cotta:
¼ cup heavy cream
½ cup granulated sugar
1 tablespoon grated ginger
1½ tablespoons powdered gelatin
6 tablespoons warm water

<u>Strawberry Sauce:</u>
2 pounds ripe strawberries, hulled
½ cup granulated sugar
2 teaspoons cornstarch
½ lemon, juice
1 pinch salt

## Preparation

1. Place the cream, sugar and ginger in a saucepan and cook over medium-low heat, until the sugar dissolves. Remove the mixture from heat and set aside.
2. In a medium-sized bowl, mix the water and the gelatin together. Set aside for a few minutes.
3. After the gelatin has rested, pour the sugar mixture into the medium-sized bowl and stir, removing all lumps.
4. Grease your ramekins and then transfer the mixture into the ramekins, leaving 2 inches of space at the top.
5. Place the ramekins in your refrigerator or freezer to let them set for *at least* 4 hours.
6. While the panna cottas are setting, make the strawberry sauce by cooking all the sauce ingredients in a medium-sized pan for 10 minutes. Stir the mixture occasionally, then remove from heat.
7. When the panna cottas are ready, flip over the containers onto a plate and allow the gelatin to stand. Drizzle with the strawberry sauce and serve.

# Applebee's Maple Butter Blondie

If you want something lighter than a brownie but just as satisfying, have a blondie. Applebee's makes them amazing, which is why we want you to be able to replicate their dish right at home.

*Serves: 6 – Preparation Time: 10 minutes – Cooking Time: 25 minutes*
*Nutrition facts per serving: Calories 1000, Total Fat 54 g, Carbs 117 g,*
*Protein 13 g, Sodium 620 mg*

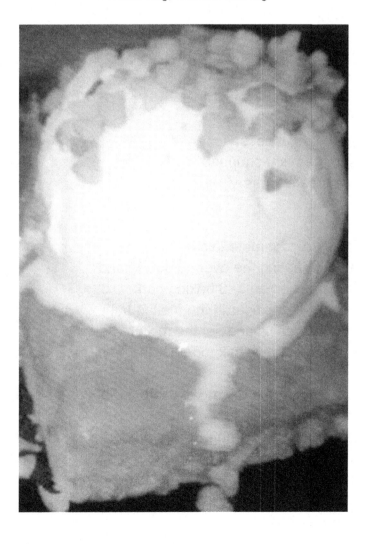

### Ingredients

⅓ cup butter, melted

1 cup brown sugar, packed

1 egg, beaten

1 tablespoon vanilla extract

1 cup all-purpose flour

½ teaspoon baking powder

⅛ teaspoon baking soda

⅛ teaspoon salt

½ cup white chocolate chips

½ cup walnuts or pecans, chopped

Maple Cream Sauce:

½ cup maple syrup

¼ cup butter

½ cup brown sugar

8 ounces cream cheese, softened

Walnuts for garnish, chopped; *optional*

Vanilla ice cream for serving

### Preparation

1. Prepare your materials by:
   a) Preheating the oven to 350°F; and
   b) Greasing an 8×8 baking pan.
2. Dissolve the sugar in the melted butter. Whip in the egg and the vanilla and set the mixture aside.
3. In another bowl, mix together the flour, baking powder and soda, and salt.
4. Slowly pour the dry mixture into the butter mixture and mix thoroughly.
5. Make sure the mixture is at room temperature before folding in the nuts and chocolate chips.
6. Transfer the mixture into the baking pan and bake for 20 to 25 minutes.

7. While waiting for the blondies to bake, combine the syrup and butter over low heat. When the butter has melted, mix in the sugar and cream cheese. Take the mixture off the heat when the cream cheese has melted, and set aside.
8. Let the blondies cool a little and then cut them into rectangles. Serve with the syrup, top with walnuts and vanilla ice cream, if desired, and serve.

# Recipe Index

# More Books by Lina Chang

If you've missed the first volume of Copycat Recipes, feel free to check it out.

Here are some of Lina Chang's other cookbooks.

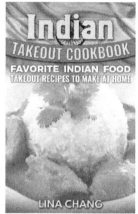

# Image Credits

# Appendix - Cooking Conversion Charts

## 1. Measuring Equivalent Chart

| Type | Imperial | Imperial | Metric |
|---|---|---|---|
| Weight | 1 dry ounce | | 28g |
| | 1 pound | 16 dry ounces | 0.45 kg |
| Volume | 1 teaspoon | | 5 ml |
| | 1 dessert spoon | 2 teaspoons | 10 ml |
| | 1 tablespoon | 3 teaspoons | 15 ml |
| | 1 Australian tablespoon | 4 teaspoons | 20 ml |
| | 1 fluid ounce | 2 tablespoons | 30 ml |
| | 1 cup | 16 tablespoons | 240 ml |
| | 1 cup | 8 fluid ounces | 240 ml |
| | 1 pint | 2 cups | 470 ml |
| | 1 quart | 2 pints | 0.95 l |
| | 1 gallon | 4 quarts | 3.8 l |
| Length | 1 inch | | 2.54 cm |

\*   Numbers are rounded to the closest equivalent

## 2. Oven Temperature Equivalent Chart

| T(°F) | T(°C) |
|-------|-------|
| 220 | 100 |
| 225 | 110 |
| 250 | 120 |
| 275 | 140 |
| 300 | 150 |
| 325 | 160 |
| 350 | 180 |
| 375 | 190 |
| 400 | 200 |
| 425 | 220 |
| 450 | 230 |
| 475 | 250 |
| 500 | 260 |

\*   T(°C) = [T(°F)-32] * 5/9

\*\*  T(°F) = T(°C) * 9/5 + 32

\*\*\* Numbers are rounded to the closest equivalent

Made in the USA
Coppell, TX
08 January 2021

47772505R00134